Stephan Timmer

Reinforcement Learning with History Lists

Stephan Timmer

Reinforcement Learning with History Lists

Solving Partially Observable Decision Processes by Using Short Term Memory

Südwestdeutscher Verlag für Hochschulschriften

Impressum/Imprint (nur für Deutschland/ only for Germany)
Bibliografische Information der Deutschen Nationalbibliothek: Die Deutsche Nationalbibliothek verzeichnet diese Publikation in der Deutschen Nationalbibliografie; detaillierte bibliografische Daten sind im Internet über http://dnb.d-nb.de abrufbar.
Alle in diesem Buch genannten Marken und Produktnamen unterliegen warenzeichen-, marken- oder patentrechtlichem Schutz bzw. sind Warenzeichen oder eingetragene Warenzeichen der jeweiligen Inhaber. Die Wiedergabe von Marken, Produktnamen, Gebrauchsnamen, Handelsnamen, Warenbezeichnungen u.s.w. in diesem Werk berechtigt auch ohne besondere Kennzeichnung nicht zu der Annahme, dass solche Namen im Sinne der Warenzeichen- und Markenschutzgesetzgebung als frei zu betrachten wären und daher von jedermann benutzt werden dürften.

Verlag: Südwestdeutscher Verlag für Hochschulschriften Aktiengesellschaft & Co. KG
Dudweiler Landstr. 99, 66123 Saarbrücken, Deutschland
Telefon +49 681 37 20 271-1, Telefax +49 681 37 20 271-0, Email: info@svh-verlag.de
Zugl.: Osnabrück, Universität Osnabrück, Dissertation, 2009

Herstellung in Deutschland:
Schaltungsdienst Lange o.H.G., Berlin
Books on Demand GmbH, Norderstedt
Reha GmbH, Saarbrücken
Amazon Distribution GmbH, Leipzig
ISBN: 978-3-8381-0621-2

Imprint (only for USA, GB)
Bibliographic information published by the Deutsche Nationalbibliothek: The Deutsche Nationalbibliothek lists this publication in the Deutsche Nationalbibliografie; detailed bibliographic data are available in the Internet at http://dnb.d-nb.de.
Any brand names and product names mentioned in this book are subject to trademark, brand or patent protection and are trademarks or registered trademarks of their respective holders. The use of brand names, product names, common names, trade names, product descriptions etc. even without a particular marking in this works is in no way to be construed to mean that such names may be regarded as unrestricted in respect of trademark and brand protection legislation and could thus be used by anyone.

Publisher:
Südwestdeutscher Verlag für Hochschulschriften Aktiengesellschaft & Co. KG
Dudweiler Landstr. 99, 66123 Saarbrücken, Germany
Phone +49 681 37 20 271-1, Fax +49 681 37 20 271-0, Email: info@svh-verlag.de

Copyright © 2009 by the author and Südwestdeutscher Verlag für Hochschulschriften Aktiengesellschaft & Co. KG and licensors
All rights reserved. Saarbrücken 2009

Printed in the U.S.A.
Printed in the U.K. by (see last page)
ISBN: 978-3-8381-0621-2

Contents

1 Introduction   **13**
    1.1 Different Ways of Learning 13
    1.2 The Actor-Critic Architecture for Agents 14
    1.3 Main Contributions and Outline 15

2 Reinforcement Learning and Abstraction   **17**
    2.1 Markov Decision Processes (MDPs) 17
    2.2 Problem Settings in Reinforcement Learning 19
    2.3 Value Iteration and Q-Learning 20
       2.3.1 Value Iteration 21
       2.3.2 Q-Learning 22
    2.4 Abstraction in Reinforcement Learning 24
       2.4.1 Existing Techniques for Creating State Abstractions in Reinforcement Learning 25

3 A Connection Between State Abstractions and POMDPs   **28**
    3.1 Abstract State Spaces and Decision Boundaries 28
       3.1.1 Generating Abstract States by Making Observations . . . 31
       3.1.2 Discussion of Observation-Based Learning 33
    3.2 Optimal Policies for General POMDPs 34
       3.2.1 Belief States and Piecewise Linear Value Functions 38
       3.2.2 Analysis of Exact Value Iteration for POMDPs 40
       3.2.3 Alternatives to the Value Iteration Algorithm 41

4 Solving POMDPs without a Model   **44**
    4.1 Different Types of Memory 45
       4.1.1 Without Memory 45
       4.1.2 History Lists and Suffix Trees 47
       4.1.3 Stochastic Finite State Controller 49
       4.1.4 Recurrent Neural Networks 50
       4.1.5 Hidden Markov Models 51
    4.2 Learning Suboptimal Policies based on Short-Term Memory . . . 52
       4.2.1 A Partially Observable Maze 53
       4.2.2 Basic Facts about History Lists 54

		4.2.3	The Identify&Exploit Algorithm	59
		4.2.4	Learning Complete History Spaces	73
		4.2.5	Empirical Analysis of Partially Observable Mazes	75
	4.3	Scaling Up the Identify&Exploit Algorithm	92
		4.3.1	An Alternative Criterion for Detecting Identifying History Lists	92
		4.3.2	Abstract States with History	100
		4.3.3	Empirical Results for the Mountain Car	106
		4.3.4	Empirical Results for the Cart-Pole	111

5 Future Work on the Identify&Exploit Algorithm   115
    5.1 Solving general POMDPs with History Lists 115
        5.1.1 Generalizations of the History List Concept 115
        5.1.2 Noisy POMDPs 116
    5.2 Performance Tuning 119
        5.2.1 Data Efficiency 119
        5.2.2 Extending the Efficient Identification Strategy 120
        5.2.3 Combining Criterion CC and Criterion CE 120
        5.2.4 Extracting Features from States 121
    5.3 Summary 121

A Proofs of Lemmas   124

B Proofs of Theorems   129

C Learning Curves for Criterion CC   138

D Learning Curves for Criterion CE   143

List of Figures

1.1 The actor-critic architecture 14

3.1 Unambiguous abstract state space The circle denotes the original state space S, while the partitioning into regions constitutes the abstract state space Z. 29
3.2 An abstract state space induced by an observation space. Each observation can be uniquely mapped to the subset of the state space in which the observation is made. The observation space consists of six distinct observations ($|O| = 6$). The resulting abstract state space is unambiguous. 32
3.3 An abstract state space induced by sequences of observations and actions. The three circles correspond to the three abstract states $z^{[o_3]}$, $z^{[o_2,a_2,o_3]}$ and $z^{[o_1,a_1,o_2,a_2,o_3]}$. The outermost circle represents the region of the state space in which observation o_3 is made ($z^{[o_3]}$). The second, more inner circle represents the subset of states, in which the process may be after making observation o_2, then executing action a_2 and finally making observation o_3 ($z^{[o_2,a_2,o_3]}$). The innermost circle represents the subset of states in which the process may be after executing the actions a_1 and a_2 and making the observations o_1, o_2, and o_3 ($z^{[o_1,a_1,o_2,a_2,o_3]}$). . 33

4.1 History lists and suffix trees. A history list consists of a single sequence of observations and actions, while a tree possibly contains several such sequences. For example, the leftmost branch of the tree shown in the figure is a prefix of the history list above. 47
4.2 Stochastic finite state controller. The figure shows a stochastic finite state controller with two nodes and two actions. In this example, the local policies are stochastic, while the state transitions are deterministic. 49
4.3 A recurrent neural network. The figure shows a network with two input units, four hidden units and one output unit. 50
4.4 Maze with partial observability 53

4.5 Components of a history list. A history list is a suffix of the complete sequence of past observations and actions (information state). The dashed observation o_{t-n} is included in the list only if the observation model f_O depends solely on the state ($f_O : S \to O$). . 55

4.6 A deterministic POMDP with three states, two actions and two observations. The observations made solely depend on the state ($f_O : S \to O$). Next to the transition graph of the POMDP, a single identifying history list is built for each state. 57

4.7 Three identifying history lists identifying the same cell in a partially observable maze. Each identifying history list is denoted by a sequence of black arrows. 57

4.8 Learning memoryless policies for the small maze by Sarsa(λ). The x-axis shows the number of control cycles, while the y-axis shows the average number of steps to the goal. The number of steps to the goal is averaged over all possible starting states. Setting of parameters: Learning rate $\alpha = 0.01$, exploration rate $\epsilon = 0.4$ (linearly decreasing), discounting rate $\beta = 1$, and $\lambda = 0.9$. 78

4.9 Learning memoryless policies for the big maze by Sarsa(λ). The x-axis shows the number of control cycles, while the y-axis shows the average number of steps to the goal. The number of steps to the goal is averaged over all possible starting states. Setting of parameters: Learning rate $\alpha = 0.01$, exploration rate $\epsilon = 0.4$ (linearly decreasing), discounting rate $\beta = 1$, and $\lambda = 0.95$. . . . 79

4.10 Three ordinary transitions compared to one abstract transition. Only a single abstract transition is created, because the first three observations of the sequence are all the same. The reward of the abstract transition equals the cumulative reward of the three single transitions. If temporal abstraction is used in such a manner, the current history list is derived from the new shorter sequence of observations and actions. 82

4.11 Policies learned for the small maze by the QU-list algorithm. The x-axis shows the number of control cycles, while the y-axis shows the average number of steps to the goal. The number of steps to the goal is averaged over all possible starting states. Setting of parameters: Learning rate $\alpha = 0.2$, constant exploration rate $\epsilon = 0.3$, discounting rate $\beta = 1$, $N_{max} = 200$ and $n_{ref} = 1000$ sampled transition instances. 83

4.12 Policies learned for the big maze by the QU-list algorithm with temporal abstraction. The x-axis shows the number of control cycles, while the y-axis shows the average number of steps to the goal. The number of steps to the goal is averaged over all possible starting states. Setting of parameters: Learning rate $\alpha = 0.1$, constant exploration rate $\epsilon = 0.1$, discounting rate $\beta = 1$, $N_{max} = 200$ and $n_{ref} = 40$ sampled episodes. 85

4.13 The Identify&Exploit algorithm applied to the small maze using criterion CC. The x-axis shows the number of control cycles, while the y-axis shows the number of steps to the goal averaged over all possible starting states. Setting of parameters: 6-complete history space, constant exploration rate $\epsilon = 0.1$, discounting rate $\beta = 1.0$, and the maximal search depth $L = 2$ (efficient identification). After every $|\mathcal{F}_{new}| = 5000$ sampled transition instances, the Q-learning update loop was executed. 89

4.14 The Identify&Exploit algorithm applied to the big maze using criterion CC. The x-axis shows the number of control cycles, while the y-axis shows the number of steps to the goal averaged over all possible starting states. Setting of parameters: 9-complete history space, constant exploration rate $\epsilon = 0.2$, discounting rate $\beta = 1.0$, and the maximal search depth $L = 2$ (efficient identification). After every $|\mathcal{F}_{new}| = 100000$ sampled transition instances, the Q-learning update loop was executed. 90

4.15 The Identify&Exploit algorithm applied to the big maze using the efficient identification strategy and criterion CC. The x-axis shows the number of control cycles, while the y-axis shows the number of steps to the goal averaged over all possible starting states. 91

4.16 The Identify&Exploit algorithm applied to the big maze using criterion CE. The x-axis shows the number of control cycles, while the y-axis shows the number of steps to the goal averaged over all possible starting states. Setting of parameters: 9-complete history space, constant exploration rate $\epsilon = 0.2$, discounting rate $\beta = 0.98$, and the maximal search depth $L = 2$ (efficient identification). After every $|\mathcal{F}| = 100000$ sampled transition instances, the Q-learning update loop was executed. 98

4.17 The Identify&Exploit algorithm applied to the big maze using the efficient identification strategy and criterion CE. The x-axis shows the number of control cycles, while the y-axis shows the number of steps to the goal averaged over all possible starting states. 99

4.18 Learning policies for the mountain car. The x-axis shows the number of control cycles, while the y-axis shows the cumulative reward achieved. Setting of parameters: Learning rate $\alpha = 0.1$, constant exploration rate $\epsilon = 0.05$, discounting rate $\beta = 0.98$. After every ten sampled episodes, the Q-learning update loop is executed with $N_{max} = 200$. After every $n_{ref} = 10000$ sampled transition instances, the history space is refined by Algorithm 8. A total number of $3*10^5$ transition instances is sampled in order to learn a policy. 108

4.19 Learning policies for the mountain car using criterion CE(0.3) to detect identifying history lists. The x-axis shows the number of control cycles, while the y-axis shows the cumulative reward achieved. The five learning curves correspond to different settings of the parameter L, the maximal search depth of the efficient identification strategy. 109

4.20 Learning policies for the mountain car using criterion CE(0.5) to detect identifying history lists. The x-axis shows the number of control cycles, while the y-axis shows the cumulative reward achieved. The five learning curves correspond to different settings of the parameter L, i.e. the maximal search depth of the efficient identification strategy. 110

4.21 Learning balancing policies for the cart-pole. The x-axis shows the number of control cycles, while the y-axis shows the cumulative reward achieved. Setting of parameters: Learning rate $\alpha = 0.1$, constant exploration rate $\epsilon = 0.1$, discounting rate $\beta = 0.98$. After every ten sampled episodes, the Q-learning update loop is executed with $N_{max} = 200$. After every $n_{ref} = 50000$ sampled transition instances, the history space is refined by Algorithm 8. A total number of $7 * 10^5$ transition instances is sampled in order to learn a policy. 112

4.22 Learning balancing policies for the cart-pole. The x-axis shows the number of control cycles, while the y-axis shows the number of steps the policy is capable of balancing the pole. 113

C.1 The Identify&Exploit algorithm applied to the big maze using criterion CC. The x-axis shows the number of control cycles, while the y-axis shows the number of steps to the goal averaged over all possible starting states. Setting of parameters: 6-complete history space, constant exploration rate $\epsilon = 0.2$, discounting rate $\beta = 1.0$, and the maximal search depth $L = 7$ (efficient identification). After every $|\mathcal{F}_{new}| = 100000$ sampled transition instances, the Q-learning update loop was executed. 138

C.2 The Identify&Exploit algorithm applied to the big maze using criterion CC. The x-axis shows the number of control cycles, while the y-axis shows the number of steps to the goal averaged over all possible starting states. Setting of parameters: 7-complete history space, constant exploration rate $\epsilon = 0.1$, discounting rate $\beta = 1.0$, and the maximal search depth $L = 4$ (efficient identification). After every $|\mathcal{F}_{new}| = 100000$ sampled transition instances, the Q-learning update loop was executed. 139

C.3 The Identify&Exploit algorithm applied to the big maze using criterion CC. The x-axis shows the number of control cycles, while the y-axis shows the number of steps to the goal averaged over all possible starting states. Setting of parameters: 8-complete history space, constant exploration rate $\epsilon = 0.2$, discounting rate $\beta = 1.0$, and the maximal search depth $L = 3$ (efficient identification). After every $|\mathcal{F}_{new}| = 100000$ sampled transition instances, the Q-learning update loop was executed. 140

C.4 The Identify&Exploit algorithm applied to the big maze using criterion CC. The x-axis shows the number of control cycles, while the y-axis shows the number of steps to the goal averaged over all possible starting states. Setting of parameters: 9-complete history space, constant exploration rate $\epsilon = 0.2$, discounting rate $\beta = 1.0$, and the maximal search depth $L = 2$ (efficient identification). After every $|\mathcal{F}_{new}| = 100000$ sampled transition instances, the Q-learning update loop was executed. 141

C.5 The Identify&Exploit algorithm applied to the big maze using the efficient identification strategy and criterion CC. The x-axis shows the number of control cycles, while the y-axis shows the number of steps to the goal averaged over all possible starting states. 142

D.1 The Identify&Exploit algorithm applied to the big maze using criterion CE. The x-axis shows the number ofcontrol cycles, while the y-axis shows the number of steps to the goal averaged over all possible starting states. Setting of parameters: 6-complete history space, constant exploration rate $\epsilon = 0.2$, discounting rate $\beta = 0.98$, and the maximal search depth $L = 3$ (efficient identification). After every $|\mathcal{F}| = 100000$ sampled transition instances, the Q-learning update loop was executed. 143

D.2 The Identify&Exploit algorithm applied to the big maze using criterion CE. The x-axis shows the number of control cycles, while the y-axis shows the number of steps to the goal averaged over all possible starting states. Setting of parameters: 7-complete history space, constant exploration rate $\epsilon = 0.1$, discounting rate $\beta = 0.98$, and the maximal search depth $L = 3$ (efficient identification). After every $|\mathcal{F}| = 100000$ sampled transition instances, the Q-learning update loop was executed. 144

D.3 The Identify&Exploit algorithm applied to the big maze using criterion CE. The x-axis shows the number of control cycles, while the y-axis shows the number of steps to the goal averaged over all possible starting states. Setting of parameters: 8-complete history space, constant exploration rate $\epsilon = 0.2$, discounting rate $\beta = 0.98$, and the maximal search depth $L = 3$ (efficient identification). After every $|\mathcal{F}| = 100000$ sampled transition instances, the Q-learning update loop was executed. 145

D.4 The Identify&Exploit algorithm applied to the big maze using criterion CE. The x-axis shows the number of control cycles, while the y-axis shows the number of steps to the goal averaged over all possible starting states. Setting of parameters: 9-complete history space, constant exploration rate $\epsilon = 0.2$, discounting rate $\beta = 0.98$, and the maximal search depth $L = 2$ (efficient identification). After every $|\mathcal{F}| = 100000$ sampled transition instances, the Q-learning update loop was executed. 146

D.5 The Identify&Exploit algorithm applied to the big maze using the efficient identification strategy and criterion CE. The x-axis shows the number of control cycles, while the y-axis shows the number of steps to the goal averaged over all possible starting states. 147

List of Tables

4.1 Possible observations in a POMDP maze. The first column gives the unique number of the observation and the second column gives the combination of walls detected by the sensors. The * symbol denotes a combination which is not present in the considered maze. 54

4.2 Possible actions in a POMDP maze. 54

4.3 Performance of optimal policies. The third column corresponds to an optimal policy for the fully observable case (MDP), while the fourth column corresponds to an optimal policy for the partially observable case (POMDP). Both columns give the number of steps to the goal averaged over every possible starting state. A state s a possible starting state if it is a non-obstacle cell. ... 76

4.4 Performance of optimal, memoryless policies. The third column gives the percentage of starting states from which the optimal policy reaches the goal state. The fourth column gives the number of steps to the goal averaged over every possible starting state. An episode for testing the learned policy is aborted if the goal state is not reached after at most 200 steps. 77

4.5 Average performance of policies learned by Sarsa(λ). The third column gives the number of steps to the goal averaged over every possible starting state. The fourth column gives the percentage of the twenty runs of Sarsa(λ), in which the optimal memoryless policy was found. An episode for testing the learned policy is aborted if the goal state is not reached after at most 200 steps. . 80

4.6 Average performance of policies learned by the QU-List algorithm. The third column gives the number of steps to the goal averaged over every possible starting state. 83

4.7 Best and worst performance of policies for the big maze learned by the QU-list algorithm with temporal abstraction. The third column gives the performance of the best run, while the fourth column gives the performance of the worst run. The performance of a policy is expressed by the average number of steps to the goal. 84

4.8 The sufficient history length of the partially observable mazes shown in Figure 4.4. The small maze consists of the lower right part of the original maze. 86

4.9 History spaces learned by Algorithm 6. The second column gives the parameter k of the algorithm. The third column gives the total size of the history space learned. The fourth column gives the number of identifying history lists from the learned space detected by criterion CC. All values shown are averaged over twenty runs. The numbers in braces give the standard deviation. All history spaces learned were actually k-complete. 87

4.10 Performance of the Identify&Exploit algorithm using criterion CC for detecting identifying history lists. The second column shows the type of history space and the third column shows the maximal search depth used by the efficient identification strategy. The fourth column shows the number of steps to the goal averaged over all possible starting states. 90

4.11 Performance of criterion CE on a 6-complete history space. The first column gives the size of the history space learned. The second column gives the percentage of correctly classified identifying history lists and the third column gives the percentage of correctly classified non-identifying history lists. All values are averaged over ten runs of the algorithm. The values given in braces denote the standard deviation. 97

4.12 Performance of the Identify&Exploit algorithm using criterion CE for detecting identifying history lists. The second column shows the type of history space used. The third column shows the number of steps to the goal averaged over all possible starting states for criterion CE. The fourth column shows the corresponding performance of criterion CC. 100

4.13 Performance of the Identify&Exploit algorithm using criterion CE on incomplete history spaces. The first column shows the size of the learned history spaces. For all three experiments, the same history spaces were used. The second column shows the number of randomly deleted history lists and the third column shows the performance of the final policies learned. All values are averaged over ten runs of the algorithm. The values given in braces denote the standard deviation. 100

4.14 Final performance of policies learned for the mountain car. The second column shows the size of the history space learned. The third column shows the setting of parameter L and the fourth column shows the averaged cumulative reward achieved. The first row shows the performance of an optimal policy. The numbers in braces give the standard deviation. 107

4.15 Final performance of policies learned for the cart-pole. The second column shows the size of the history spaces learned. The third column shows the number of steps the final policy is capable of balancing the pole and the fourth column shows the cumulative reward achieved by the final policy. The numbers in braces give the standard deviation. 112

List of Algorithms

1	Q-Learning	24
2	Value Iteration for POMDPs	40
3	Identify and Exploit	61
4	Safe Q-Learning on History Lists	62
5	Efficient Identification	63
6	Learning k-Complete History Spaces	74
7	Sarsa(λ)	77
8	Refinement of History Space	81
9	QU-List	82
10	Q-Learning with Criterion CE(δ)	104
11	Q-Learning with MaxProb	105

Chapter 1

Introduction

1.1 Different Ways of Learning

Algorithms from the field of machine learning aim at improving their performance by constantly evaluating experience gathered. Experience can be either given in advance in the form of a data stream or it must be obtained by an exploration strategy. Since learning from experience is one of the most important aspects of intelligent behavior, machine learning is regarded as a subfield of artificial intelligence.

This thesis is concerned with model-free reinforcement learning, which is somewhat in between the two poles of machine learning, namely supervised learning and unsupervised learning.

Supervised Learning In supervised learning, the learner is provided with a certain kind of feedback after making decisions. In particular, the feedback informs the learner about the decisions that would have been correct. This information can be used by the learner to improve the quality of future decisions.

Unsupervised Learning In unsupervised learning, there is nothing like a teacher giving feedback to the learner. Thus, the learner must solve the problem solely by exploiting similarities and regularities given in the available data.

Reinforcement Learning In reinforcement learning, there is feedback similar to supervised learning, but it contains less information. In contrast to supervised learning, the feedback does not include the correct decisions, but only hints in the form of rewards and penalties. The quality of a decision is reflected in how much reward it provides the learner. Thus, the learner improves his performance by memorizing the outcome of different decisions and adapting his behavior accordingly.

1.2 The Actor-Critic Architecture for Agents

"Don't ask, I'm an agent."
Gary Numan, "Telekon", 1980

In reinforcement learning, the learner is viewed as an agent interacting with an environment by executing actions. Decisions therefore correspond to action choices and rewards are given in response to those action choices. Since the agent concept constitutes a valid framework for artificial intelligence in general, we refer to the well-known definition of an agent from [RN03]:

> "An agent is anything that can be viewed as perceiving its environment through sensors and acting upon that environment through actuators."

As an amendment to this definition, it is widely accepted in machine learning to consider only rational agents. A rational agent tries to take an optimal action with respect to the knowledge currently available. Such a conditionally optimal action differs significantly from the globally optimal action, which would be desirable to know, but may be impossible to derive from the experience accessible to the agent.

The actor-critic model from [SB98] shown in Figure 1.1 is a special architecture for rational agents and constitutes the basis for almost all reinforcement learning algorithms as well as for this thesis. The agent consists of two distinct

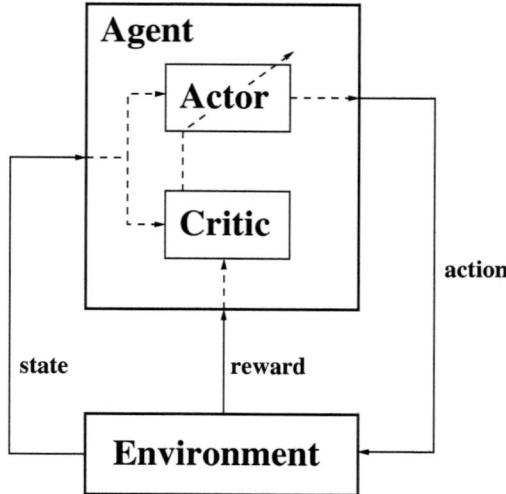

Figure 1.1: The actor-critic architecture

modules, which are named the actor and the critic. While the actor is responsible for executing actions by controlling the actuators of the agent, the critic maintains an internal representation of the environment. This representation is used for ranking the different actions with respect to their success in solving the learning problem. The rewards gained from the environment serve as a performance measure necessary for quantifying the success of an action. Thus, to evaluate the effects of an action in different environmental states, the action must be executed several times on a trial and error basis. This will enable the critic to control the learning process by giving advice to the actor as to which action should be executed in a certain state. The critic therefore defines the policy of the agent.

The environment responds to an action choice of the agent by both emitting a scalar reward and making a transition to a next environmental state. The new state information is captured by the agent through its sensors and forwarded both to the actor and the critic. The most important part of a reinforcement learning algorithm is located in the critic section of the agent. The task of the critic is complex for several reasons. First, the set of states for which different actions must be ranked is possibly very large. Moreover, it does not suffice to judge each action separately. To solve typical reinforcement learning problems, it is necessary to execute several actions constituting a sequence of decisions. The critic therefore has to analyze the dependencies that may exist within an action sequence. For example, some actions may be only useful when executed early in the sequence, while others should be executed at the end. It is also possible that an action is only successful in combination with other actions. This problem is called the temporal-credit assignment problem.

Note that a trial and error procedure of choosing actions, as described above, is only needed for the model-free case. If the learning agent has access to prior knowledge about the environment in the form of a model predicting the outcome of an action, the learning problem changes into a planning problem. Solving a planning problem does not require any interaction with the environment. The algorithms developed in this thesis are all model-free, i.e. without using any form of prior knowledge.

1.3 Main Contributions and Outline

A still open problem in reinforcement learning is how to scale existing algorithms to infinite possibly continuous state spaces. This is particularly true for the model-free case, in which the learning agent is left with no prior knowledge about the environment. To solve this problem, it is necessary to introduce some form of abstraction allowing generalization over states. Since there exists a straightforward connection between state abstractions and partially observable Markov decision processes (POMDPs), model-free algorithms for solving POMDPs can also be applied to fully observable Markov decision processes (MDPs) with continuous state spaces. The main contribution of this thesis is the development of a novel, model-free algorithm for POMDPs. In a first step, we apply this algorithm to a typical POMDP benchmark with a finite number of states. By making use of state abstractions, we then modify the algorithm such that it becomes applicable also for MDPs with continuous state spaces. The algorithms will be analyzed and discussed both from a theoretical as well as from an empirical point of view.

We will now give a brief outline of the thesis. The second chapter introduces the basic concepts and algorithms from the field of reinforcement learning. Various mechanisms for including abstraction into reinforcement learning are discussed and then related to the problem of reducing a continuous state space.

The third chapter formally states a definition of an abstract state space and analyzes how abstract state spaces are connected to POMDPs. We will motivate our work by showing that an abstract state space can be perfectly represented by the observation space of a POMDP. We then discuss algorithms already available for solving POMDPs. A severe limitation of current POMDP algorithms is that most algorithms are model-based, i.e. the complete model needs to be known in advance in order to compute a policy.

The fourth chapter presents a novel model-free algorithm for POMDPs based on the use of history lists. History lists are sequences of past observations and actions constituting a form of short-term memory. The algorithm developed is designed for deterministic systems, although the basic idea carries over to the stochastic case. In the first part of the fourth chapter, the algorithm is evaluated on a maze problem having a finite number of cells. The second part of the fourth chapter is concerned with extending the algorithm such that it becomes applicable to typical continuous reinforcement learning benchmarks like, for example, cart-pole balancing. This is achieved by exploiting the formerly stated connection between POMDPs and abstract state spaces.

The fifth chapter presents possible extensions of our algorithm, both by tuning the performance as well as by generalizing the history list concept. In particular, we will discuss how to scale our algorithm to the general stochastic case.

The main contributions of this thesis can be summarized as follows:

1. Development of a novel model-free algorithm for POMDPs.

2. Making a connection between POMDPs and abstractions over states. Such a connection significantly simplifies learning problems with continuous state spaces.

Chapter 2

Reinforcement Learning and Abstraction

The formal framework used in reinforcement learning for specifying learning problems as well as solutions to these problems is provided by the theory about Markov decision processes (MDPs). The components of the actor-critic model described in the introduction can be mapped to the components of a corresponding Markov decision process (MDP).

2.1 Markov Decision Processes (MDPs)

A Markov decision process is a special case of a stochastic process in which state transitions are statistically independent from past transitions. This property is also called the Markov property. If the sequence of actions carried out by the learning agent is fixed, an MDP reduces to a simple Markov chain.

Definition 1. *Markov Decision Process (MDP)*
A Markov decision process $M := (T, S, A, P_S, r)$ is a five-tuple consisting of a discrete set of time steps T, a set of states S, a set of finite actions A, a probabilistic transition model P_S, and a reward function $r : S \times A \to \mathbb{R}$.

At every time $t \in T$, the process is in a certain state $s_t \in S$. After an action $a_t \in A$ is executed, a scalar reward $r(s_t, a_t)$ is emitted and a stochastic transition to another state s_{t+1} occurs. The transition model P_S can be represented by matrices P_S^a for all actions $a \in A$, such that an element $p_{ss'}^a \in P_S^a$ denotes the probability of a state transition from $s \in S$ to $s' \in S$ after executing action $a \in A$. Alternatively, this probability can be written as $P_S(s' \mid s, a)$. If the set of time steps T is finite, an additional terminal reward[1] $r(s_{T_F}, \cdot)$ independent of action is given at the last time step $T_F \in T$.

---

[1] In order to keep the notational requirements at a minimum, we will not introduce an extra function $R : S \to \mathbb{R}$ for expressing the terminal reward.

Definition 2. *Deterministic Markov Decision Process*
A deterministic Markov decision process $M := (T, S, A, P_S, r)$ is a Markov decision process such that the transition model P_S can be replaced by a deterministic function $f_S : S \times A \to S$. The function f_S gives for every state $s \in S$ and action $a \in A$ a uniquely defined successor state $s' \in S$. For the deterministic case, the MDP can also be written as $M := (T, S, A, f_S, r)$.

It is possible to consider even more general MDPs, for example by allowing continuous action spaces. However, in this work, all considered problem settings will fit into the restrictive framework defined above.

When relating the actor-critic model to an MDP, it is instructive to think of the following analogies:

Environment The environment is represented by the state of the process. We assume that the learning agent is equipped with various types of sensors to observe the current state of the environment. The transition probabilities $P_S(s' \mid s, a)$ model how the environment changes when the agent executes actions.

Actor The actor, i.e. the learning agent, has control over the actions executed at every time step. The agent therefore tries to alter the state of the environment according to the given task specification.

Critic The critic is closely related to the reward signals. In particular, the reward signals serve as a feedback to the critic part of the learning agent. A low reward indicates that the last action was a bad action, whereas a high reward indicates that the last action was successful. The agent learns to select actions by being encouraged or punished in the form of reward signals. For this purpose, the critic memorizes past rewards and ranks (criticizes) different actions according to how much reward they provided.

In reinforcement learning, the reward is usually regarded as part of the environment. This is due to historical reasons and has a lot to do with how the field of reinforcement learning originated from other disciplines, such as psychology or operations research. In [SB98], a detailed discussion about these issues is provided. To summarize, the critic gives advice to the learning agent about what actions lead to successful behavior. This advice is based on the reward provided by the environment.

The goal of the learning agent is to maximize the cumulative reward on a sequence of state transitions. Thus, the reward function implicitly defines the learning problem. The idea of reinforcement learning is that the agent learns successful behavior by a trial and error procedure of selecting different actions. In the context of reinforcement learning, the behavior of an agent is called a policy.

Definition 3. *Policies for Markov Decision Processes*
Let $M := (T, S, A, P_S, r)$ be a Markov decision process. A policy for M is a set of mappings $\pi := \{\pi_t\}_{(t \in T)}$ such that each mapping $\pi_t : S \to A$ can be interpreted as a rule for choosing actions at time $t \in T$. Such a policy is called non-stationary, since the policy may change over time. If $\forall t \in T, \forall t' \in T : \pi_t = \pi_{t'}$, then the set of mappings reduces to a single stationary policy $\pi : S \to A$.

The set Π denotes the space of all possible policies, including both non-stationary policies as well as stationary policies.

By trying out different policies, the agent should eventually arrive at an optimal policy. This optimal policy is defined by maximizing over the expected sum of discounted rewards.

Definition 4. *Optimal Policies for Markov Decision Processes*
Let $M := (T, S, A, P_S, r)$ be a Markov decision process and let $0 \le \beta \le 1$ be a discounting factor. First, consider the case of a finite set of time steps T such that $T_F \in T$ is the maximal element of T. A policy $\pi^* := \{\pi_t^*\}_{(t \in T)}$ is called optimal with respect to M, if
$\pi^* \in \arg\max_{\pi \in \Pi} E[\sum_{t=0}^{T_F - 1} \beta^t\, r(s_t, \pi_t(s_t)) + \beta^{T_F} r(s_{T_F}, \cdot)]$.

If the set of time steps T is infinite, then a policy $\pi^* := \{\pi_t^*\}_{(t \in T)}$ is called optimal with respect to M, if $\pi^* \in \arg\max_{\pi \in \Pi} E[\sum_{t=0}^{\infty} \beta^t\, r(s_t, \pi_t(s_t))]$.

As we will see later, optimal policies do not depend on the initial state $s_0 \in S$ of the process if the set of time steps T is infinite. The above definition of optimal policies is therefore useful, given an arbitrary procedure for selecting initial states.

2.2 Problem Settings in Reinforcement Learning

The goal of every reinforcement learning algorithm is to find an optimal policy as fast as possible. How fast an algorithm actually is can be measured by the number of interactions with the environment, i.e. the number of actions executed.

However, it is not always possible to directly compare different learning algorithms, because they address different types of problems. To sort this work into the stream of research, we will summarize the most important features of typical reinforcement learning problems.

Model The transition probabilities P_S and the reward function r are called the model of an MDP. If a learning algorithm uses knowledge about the model, it is called model-based. Obviously, information about the model considerably helps the learning agent to solve a problem. If no such information is available, the algorithm is called model-free. Algorithms developed in this thesis are all model-free. However, we will also analyze some important model-based algorithms.

System Dynamics In general, state transitions of a Markov process are stochastic. However, if the transition probabilities can be expressed by a deterministic function f_S, the learning problem is called deterministic. In this thesis, most problem settings will be deterministic, although we will discuss how to scale to the stochastic case.

Observability In order to introduce state abstractions into reinforcement learning, we will consider extensions of the MDP framework dealing with partial observability. A POMDP is an extension of an MDP in the sense that the learning agent can make only observations of the current state. These observations do not fully reveal the state and therefore prune information about the state. The algorithms developed in the fourth chapter concentrate on techniques for coping with partial observability. It will turn out that these techniques constitute a form of state abstraction which can also be used for MDPs.

Size The size of a reinforcement learning problem is basically determined by the size of the state space. In this work, we will consider both finite state spaces as well as continuous multi-dimensional ones.

Horizon If the set of time steps T is finite, the process terminates after a finite number of state transitions. In such a setting, the learning problem is called a finite horizon problem and the policies considered are non-stationary. In the case of an infinite horizon, the optimal policy is stationary. A proof of this assertion will follow in the next section. All algorithms developed in this thesis learn stationary policies, since we assume an infinite horizon.

Agent A problem may require several agents cooperating to achieve a shared goal. It is also possible that agents have different goals and therefore compete with each other. These problems are called multi-agent problems. However, in this work, we will only consider single agents as illustrated in the actor-critic model.

This thesis concentrates on model-free algorithms for deterministic POMDPs. However, the techniques developed will also be used to solve MDPs by introducing state abstractions. The next chapter provides a detailed discussion about state abstractions and what can they can be used for.

2.3 Value Iteration and Q-Learning

Most reinforcement learning algorithms, especially the novel algorithms developed in this thesis, are based on two well-known standard algorithms. The value iteration procedure is by far the most important model-based algorithm, while Q-learning is the standard algorithm for solving problems without a model, i.e. model-free. The concepts introduced by these algorithms will be of great importance throughout the thesis. We will therefore shortly present the basic ideas of value iteration and Q-learning and also provide some theoretical background.

2.3.1 Value Iteration

The value iteration procedure goes back to an approach from dynamic programming [Ber01]. The basic idea of value iteration is to compute an optimal policy by solving a system of linear equations. Note that such a procedure does not require any interaction with the environment, since a model of the environment is assumed to be known. Since value iteration is model-based, all quantities needed to formally state the system of equations are given in advance.

We first consider a finite horizon such that $T_F \in T$ is a maximal element of T. Thus, after T_F state transitions, or equivalently after T_F action choices, the process terminates[2]. Note that at the last time step $t = T_F$, the learning agent is not able to execute any action.

The expected sum of discounted rewards gained by an optimal policy from the n-th step until termination is expressed by a value function $V_n : S \to \mathbb{R}$. The parameter n can take on any value from the closed interval $[0, T_F]$.

$$V_n(s) := \max_{\pi^{(n)}} E[\sum_{t=n}^{T_F-1} \beta^{t-n} r(s_t, \pi_t(s_t)) + \beta^{T_F-n} r(s_{T_F}, \cdot) \mid s_n = s] \quad (2.1)$$

The symbol $\pi^{(n)} := \{\pi_t\}_{(n \leq t < T_F)}$ denotes a non-stationary policy selecting actions from time $t = n$ until time $t = T_F - 1$. Note that for $n = 0$, the value function $V_n(s)$ equals the cumulative reward gained by an optimal policy given by Definition 4. Since the value function expresses the value of an optimal policy, the expectation is maximized over all possible policies.

The key idea of the value iteration procedure is that Equation (2.1) can be rewritten such that it constitutes a Bellman equation. It is then possible to compute the value functions V_n ($0 \leq n \leq T_F$) by a procedure from dynamic programming.

Lemma 1. *Let $M := (T, S, A, P_S, r)$ be a Markov decision process such that T is a finite set of time steps including a maximal element $T_F \in T$. A countable state space S is assumed and a discounting rate $0 \leq \beta < 1$. The value functions $V_n : S \to \mathbb{R}$ ($0 \leq n < T_F$) defined in Equation (2.1) can be equivalently expressed as follows:*

$$V_n(s) = \max_{a \in A}[r(s,a) + \beta \sum_{s' \in S} P_S(s'|s,a) V_{n+1}(s')] \quad (2.2)$$

A proof of Lemma 1 can be found in the appendix. Value iteration consists of repeatedly computing a new value function V_n from V_{n+1} by Equation (2.2). The algorithm is initialized by the trivial value function $V_{T_F}(s) = r(s, \cdot)$ at the terminal stage $n = T_F$. The first iteration of the algorithm is performed for $n = T_F - 1$. An optimal policy $\pi^* := \{\pi_0^*, ..., \pi_{T_F-1}^*\}$ can be extracted from

---
[2]We assume that counting of time steps begins at $t = 0$.

the sequence of value functions by selecting those actions yielding the maximal cumulative reward.

$$\forall s \in S: \quad \pi_n^*(s) := \arg\max_{a \in A}[r(s,a) + \beta \sum_{s' \in S} P_S(s' \mid s, a)V_{n+1}(s')] \quad (2.3)$$

Consider now an infinite horizon problem for which it holds that T_F goes to infinity ($T_F \to \infty$). The process of iterating Equation (2.2) infinitely often is equivalent to repeatedly applying an operator W defined on functions of the form $V : S \to \mathbb{R}$.

$$W[V](s) := \max_{a \in A}[r(s,a) + \beta \sum_{s' \in S} P_S(s' \mid s, a)V(s')] \quad (2.4)$$

We can state that operator W has as a unique fixed point due to the fixed point theorem of Banach. For this to show, it is sufficient to prove that W is a contraction mapping.

$$\begin{aligned} \|W[X] - W[Y]\|_\infty &= \sup_{a \in A, s \in S}[\beta \sum_{s' \in S} P_S(s' \mid s, a)(X(s') - Y(s'))] \\ &\leq \sup_{s' \in S}[\beta(X(s') - Y(s'))] \\ &= \beta\|X - Y\|_\infty \end{aligned} \quad (2.5)$$

Let $V^* : S \to \mathbb{R}$ be the uniquely defined fixed point of W, i.e. $W[V^*] = V^*$. We can see from Equation (2.4) that computing the fixed point V^* is equivalent to solving a system of $|S|$ linear equations with $|S|$ unknown variables. Fortunately, Banach's theorem guarantees that the sequence of value functions generated by applying operator W converges to V^*. Thus, the optimal value function V^* can be approximated with arbitrary precision after a finite number of iterations. In [Ber01], a complete analysis also for the undiscounted case is provided, i.e. for $\beta = 1$.

Consider now the problem of extracting an optimal policy from V^*. We assume that the optimal value function V^* is available and operator W is applied on V^* for an infinite number of times. Since V^* is a fixed point of W, the policies extracted from the resulting sequence of value functions are pairwise equivalent. It follows that the optimal policy π^* is stationary and can be extracted from Equation (2.3), if V_{n+1} is replaced by V^*. This also shows that for an infinite horizon problem, an optimal policy does not depend on the initial state of the process.

2.3.2 Q-Learning

The Q-learning algorithm is similar to value iteration since both approaches exploit the Bellman Equation (2.2) to compute a policy. However, the main difference is that Q-learning is designed to find a policy even if the model of the environment is not known in advance. Thus, it is not possible to compute the value function by a procedure from dynamic programming as it is done for value iteration.

Instead of iterating Equation (2.2), Q-learning learns a state-action value function by an approach from stochastic approximation. The approximated function is called the Q-function. Here, we only consider the case of an infinite horizon problem.

$$Q^* : S \times A \to \mathbb{R}, \; Q^*(s,a) := r(s,a) + \beta \sum_{s' \in S} P_S(s' \mid s, a) V^*(s') \qquad (2.6)$$

Note that by Equation (2.2), it holds

$$V^*(s) = \max_{a \in A} Q^*(s,a) \qquad (2.7)$$

If the Q-function Q^* is available, it is easily possible to extract an optimal policy for a state by selecting an action which maximizes the cumulative reward. Such an action is called a greedy action.

$$\forall s \in S : \; \pi^*(s) = \arg\max_{a \in A} Q^*(s,a) \qquad (2.8)$$

From Equation (2.6) and Equation (2.8), it follows that the Q-function can be rewritten in a recursive form.

$$Q^* : S \times A \to \mathbb{R}, \; Q^*(s,a) := r(s,a) + \beta \sum_{s' \in S} P_S(s' \mid s, a) \max_{a' \in A} Q^*(s', a') \qquad (2.9)$$

The Q-learning algorithm performs a stochastic approximation of the Q-function stated in Equation (2.9). This is accomplished by sampling a number of state transitions as shown in Algorithm 1. Thus, Q-learning learns from experience gathered by interaction with the environment. The algorithm was originally proposed in [Wat89]. To simplify the pseudocode of the algorithm, we assume a single, never ending episode starting at time $t = 0$. However, for most practical problem settings, it is necessary to sample several episodes, each of finite length.

Some modules of the Q-learning algorithm stated in Algorithm 1 are not fully specified because there are a variety of possible implementations, each tuned for a specific problem setting. These modules are still the subject of research and can be viewed as separate algorithms.

The action choices made by the agents serve the purpose of collecting relevant information about the environment. By trying out different actions leading to different parts of the state space, the agent implicitly learns the model of the MDP. This kind of action selection is called exploration. However, it is also important to exploit already available knowledge by selecting greedy actions with respect to the learned Q-function. Executing greedy actions is necessary because the learning process should concentrate on the parts of the state space relevant for solving the problem. Unnecessary updates of the Q-function should be avoided. Finding the optimal tradeoff between exploration and exploitation

Algorithm 1 Q-Learning

1: $\forall a \in A, \forall s \in S : \hat{Q}(s,a) \leftarrow 0$
2: $t \leftarrow 0$
3: Select initial state s_0
4: Select initial learning rate $0 < \alpha_0 \leq 1$
5: **repeat**
6:     Select action a_t in state s_t
7:     Observe reward $r_t \leftarrow r(s_t, a_t)$ and next state s_{t+1}
8:     Update Q-function:
    $\hat{Q}(s_t, a_t) \leftarrow (1-\alpha_t)\hat{Q}(s_t, a_t) + \alpha_t(r_t + \beta \max_{a \in A} \hat{Q}(s_{t+1}, a))$
9:     Update learning rate $\alpha_{t+1} \leftarrow h(\alpha_t)$
10:     $t \leftarrow t + 1$
11: **until** the Q-function converges or t exceeds a certain threshold

is a goal shared by all reinforcement learning algorithms. An example for a popular exploration strategy is the ϵ-greedy strategy, which selects a random action with probability $\epsilon > 0$ and a greedy action otherwise. This exploration strategy will be used throughout the thesis.

The learning rate α_t controls how new information about the environment affects the currently learned Q-function. The standard procedure for updating the learning rate is to incrementally decrease the rate at every time step. Thus, the agent eventually stops learning and the Q-learning procedure can be terminated. Theorem 1 gives some advice on how to choose the update function h.

Theorem 1. *Let $M := (T, S, A, P_S, r)$ be a Markov decision process such that S is a finite state space. Let $0 \leq \beta < 1$ be a discounting rate. Consider a sequence of Q-learning updates using the learning rates $\alpha_{(t)}$ and the discounting rate β such that every state-action pair from $(S \times A)$ is updated infinitely often. If $\sum_{t=0}^{\infty} \alpha_t = \infty$ and $\sum_{t=0}^{\infty} \alpha_t^2 < \infty$, then the learned Q-factors $\hat{Q}(s,a)$ converge to the optimal Q-factors $Q^*(s,a)$ for all states $s \in S$ and actions $a \in A$.*

A proof of Theorem 1 can be found in [BT96]. If some additional assumptions are made, it is also possible to prove that Q-learning converges without discounting, i.e. for $\beta = 1$.

2.4 Abstraction in Reinforcement Learning

Since this thesis concentrates on the model-free case, we want to discuss a certain limitation of the Q-learning algorithm described above. For reasonably small problems, i.e. problems with a finite number of states, Q-learning works very well. For such problem settings, there are theoretical results available, guaranteeing convergence to an optimal policy (Theorem 1). However, practical problems often have continuous or at least countably infinite state spaces.

To illustrate how severe this problem actually is, consider the case of a real-valued and multi-dimensional state space. The size of such a state space grows exponentially with the number of dimensions. This fact was named the curse of dimensionality since it prevents the standard reinforcement learning algorithms from being efficient for very large state spaces.

In reinforcement learning, dealing with large state spaces means carefully balancing exploration and exploitation. However, if the state space is infinite, it is impossible to visit every single state at least once. This remains true even if exploration is concentrated on the most important parts of the state space. Thus, it is necessary to infer the Q-values of an unvisited state from the Q-values of states actually visited. This inference can be viewed as the basic form of abstraction over states.

The idea we will follow in this thesis is to generate state abstractions by making observations of states. An observation of a state contains some information about the state, but prunes away a large portion of the original state description. For example, consider a grid that is laid over a continuous state space. The cell in which a certain state is falling, can be interpreted as an observation of this state. In other words, the state is perceived by the learning agent at a lower resolution. The next chapter will analyze in detail the connection between state abstractions and observations. This will motivate the development of model-free algorithms for POMDPs working on observation spaces. A possible generalization of our approach is to consider observations to be features extracted from a state. There are sophisticated algorithms available for extracting features, which allow to pre-process the state information. However, since we want to concentrate on reinforcement learning in this thesis, the observation spaces we will use are very simple and intuitive.

In fact, there is a variety of methods available for implementing state abstractions in reinforcement learning. Abstractions over states are often caused by other forms of abstraction, for example, temporal abstraction or hierarchical decomposition of problems. Although this work concentrates solely on state abstractions, we will give a short overview of other mechanisms of abstraction in the next subsection.

2.4.1 Existing Techniques for Creating State Abstractions in Reinforcement Learning

Function Approximation

State abstractions exploit similarities between states. If two states are similar with respect to a certain criterion, it may be advantageous to choose the same action in both states. If a Q-function is used to extract a greedy policy, then the meaning of similarity is implicitly defined by the way the Q-function is approximated. For example, if the Q-function is approximated by a k-nearest neighbor approach in a euclidean space, then two states are similar if their euclidean distance is small. This points out the primary source of state abstractions in model-free reinforcement learning: Abstractions mostly emerge due to a choice of a certain type of function approximator. Popular function approximators in reinforcement learning are grids [MM02], trees ([Rey00], [EGW05]), CMACs ([Sut96], [TR07a]), various forms of neural networks ([LM92], [Bak01], [Rie05]) or linear models defined on basis functions [LP03].

Hierarchical Reinforcement Learning

A more intuitive form of state abstraction is used in algorithms from hierarchical reinforcement learning. Here, the overall learning problem is divided into subproblems such that the states can be grouped into clusters corresponding to these subproblems. The best known approaches using this technique are the MAXQ decomposition of the value function [Die00] and the abstract machines from [PR97]. For these algorithms to work, it is necessary to impose a structure on the problem, thereby introducing prior knowledge. After a problem hierarchy is properly defined, reinforcement learning can be used to solve the subproblems in an order respecting the dependencies between the subproblems. One benefit of such a procedure is that while solving a subproblem, only a small fraction of the state space has to be considered. Moreover, a solution to a subproblem can be reused in other similar subproblems.

Temporal Abstraction

Closely related to state abstraction is temporal abstraction. A simple form of temporal abstraction is the extension of primitive actions to multi-step actions [SR02]. In contrast to primitive actions, a multi-step action is applied for several consecutive time steps. The benefit of multi-step actions is that the number of necessary decisions (action choices) can be significantly reduced. Thus, temporal abstraction leads to an acceleration of the learning process. As a side effect, state abstractions are introduced, since only a small number of states is considered in order to infer a policy. The best known approach for temporal abstraction is the options framework from [SPS99]. An option is a subpolicy restricted to a certain region of the state space. If the agent leaves this region, the execution of the option is terminated and a new option is activated. Since options are treated the same way as primitive actions, an option serves as a multi-step action possibly solving complex tasks. State abstractions appear in the options framework in the form of regions of the state space in which a certain set of options can be activated.

Relational Reinforcement Learning

A recent development in reinforcement learning is the symbolic modeling of a learning problem, for example by dynamic Bayesian nets [BP96] or by expressions from first order logic ([DRB98], [GDR03]). This field of research is named relational reinforcement. The basic idea of relational reinforcement learning is to represent the state space by a set of predicates. The standard algorithms from reinforcement learning must then be adjusted to such a symbolic representation. The use of symbols leads to a very compact representation of the state space and therefore constitutes a form of state abstraction. Interestingly, this is somewhat similar to the approach followed in this thesis, since an observation of a state can also be represented by a predicate defined on the state. However, the learning algorithms presented in this work are fundamentally different from relational reinforcement learning. While in relational reinforcement learning, the problem is represented on an abstract, symbolic level, we will formulate the learning problem as a partially observable Markov decision process (POMDP).

Chapter 3

A Connection Between State Abstractions and POMDPs

Although the use of state abstraction in reinforcement learning seems to be a crucial factor for solving complex problems, it is not clear how to actually implement such abstractions. In this chapter, we discuss the most important issues concerning abstract state spaces. In particular, we introduce a formal framework for abstract state spaces based on POMDPs.

1. What is an abstract state space?
2. What kind of policies can be defined on an abstract state space?
3. How is it possible to represent state abstraction by a partially observable Markov Decision Process (POMDP)?

3.1 Abstract State Spaces and Decision Boundaries

As already discussed in the last chapter, a variety of different types of abstractions is available in the field of reinforcement learning. In this work, we will concentrate solely on the case in which the original state space is divided into a set of regions, which are then called abstract states.

Definition 5. *Abstract State Space*
Let $M := (T, S, A, P_S, r)$ be a Markov Decision Process. An abstract state space $Z := \{z_i \mid z_i \subseteq S, 1 \leq i \leq N\}$ is a finite set of abstract states such that $\bigcup_{i=1}^{N} z_i = S$. An abstract state space Z is called unambiguous if the abstract states form disjoint sets such that $z_i \cap z_j = \emptyset$ for all pairs $(z_i, z_j) \in (Z \times Z)$ with $i \neq j$.

It is easy to see that for an unambiguous abstract state space, a policy can be defined by simply assigning an action to every abstract state. In Figure 3.1, such a space is illustrated. However, as we will show later, it is also possible to define policies on ambiguous abstract state spaces.

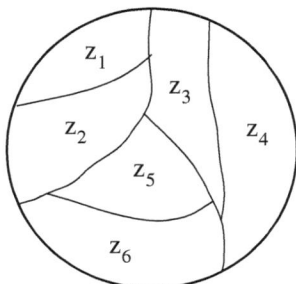

Figure 3.1: Unambiguous abstract state space The circle denotes the original state space S, while the partitioning into regions constitutes the abstract state space Z.

The basic motivation of building an abstract state space is to partition the original state space S into regions such that in every single state of a region, the same action is optimal. If these regions can be represented efficiently, then also an optimal policy can be represented efficiently. The boundaries of such regions are called decision boundaries, because they separate sets of states having different optimal actions. The first step in creating an abstract state space is therefore to find the decision boundaries and then to partition the state space accordingly. In fact, there is some work available concerned with finding decision boundaries and learning policies on the resulting abstract state spaces.

In a reinforcement learning setting, the goal is to learn both an abstract state space as well as a policy defined on this space. This is usually done by learning a value function or a Q-function. An alternative approach without using value functions is to directly search in the space of abstract policies. A discussion about policy search techniques is deferred to the end of this chapter, since these techniques do not provide further insight about abstract state spaces and are of minor interest in this work.

One of the first ideas for learning a Q-function on abstract state spaces is the Parti-Game algorithm [Moo95], in which abstract states are represented by cells of a grid. The grid covers the continuous, possibly multi-dimensional original state space S. A policy is learned by an algorithm from dynamic programming very similar to value iteration. The optimization criterion aims at minimizing the number of steps to a certain goal state. If necessary, the abstract state space is refined by splitting the grid cells into several subcells.

In [MM02], abstract states are represented by the leaves of a kd-tree and a value function is approximated using a triangulation technique. Several splitting criteria for refining the abstract state space are derived and their benifits and drawbacks are discussed. The basic idea employed for refining the abstract states is based on the influence an abstract state has on neighboring abstract states. For example, if the value of an abstract state z_1 is very much influenced by the value of another abstract state z_2, it is reasonable to increase the accuracy of the value computed for z_2. In order to achieve this, abstract state z_2 is split and the abstract state space is refined. The concept of influence is a generalization of the principal ideas from the prioritized sweeping algorithm [MA93].

A similar approach, again by using kd-trees, is implemented in [Rey00] but with a different splitting heuristic. An abstract state is split if the optimal actions of neighboring abstract states significantly differ with respect to their approximated Q-values.

For a comparison of different types of trees that can be used to partition the state space, the work in [EGW05] provides a detailed empirical evaluation. A theoretical analysis of finding decision boundaries by partitioning the state space is given in [DG97].

Unfortunately, all algorithms for learning policies on abstract state spaces suffer from similar problems. The following enumeration summarizes the reasons why the approaches described above may fail to learn optimal policies.

1. In general, the shape of the decision boundaries can be arbitrarily complex and therefore it may be hard to find those boundaries. For example, consider a problem for which some areas of the state space must be represented at a very high resolution. In such a case, the complexity of representing an abstract state space reflecting the decision boundaries has almost the same complexity as representing the original state space. Ideally, the abstract space is given by a small number of abstract states which can be efficiently stored. Most practical algorithms for learning abstract states spaces therefore do not aim at learning a perfect abstract space, but rather one on which reasonably good policies can be defined. It strongly depends on the shape of the decision boundaries whether an algorithm implementing a specific technique of representing an abstract state space will be successful or not.

2. Even if the decision boundaries can be efficiently determined such that a perfect abstract state space is available, it is not clear how to learn an optimal policy with respect to this space. Traditional reinforcement learning algorithms such as value iteration or Q-learning do not fully apply for abstract state spaces, because abstract spaces usually violate the Markov assumption. The standard algorithms are not guaranteed to find an optimal policy. In fact, value iteration and Q-learning may not even converge to a policy at all. Due to the lack of alternative algorithms, Q-learning is often used as a heuristic in such cases.

Another problem with abstract state spaces is that a policy defined on abstract states may not be able to achieve the same performance compared to an optimal policy defined on single states. Thus, the meaning of optimality changes in the context of abstract state spaces. It is not clear how algorithms should deal with this fact.

3.1.1 Generating Abstract States by Making Observations

One of the main ideas of this work is to reformulate the problem of building an abstract state space by making a straightforward connection to another field of research. This will enable us to analyze state abstractions within a formal framework being in use over a long period of time.

In this work, abstract state spaces will be represented by observations of a partially observable Markov decision process.

Definition 6. *Partially Observable Markov Decision Process (POMDP)*
A partially observable Markov decision process $M := (T, S, A, O, P_S, P_O, r)$ is a seven-tuple consisting of a Markov decision process (T, S, A, P_S, r), a finite set of observations O and a stochastic observation model P_O. The term $P_O(o \mid s, a)$ denotes the probability of making observation $o \in O$ of state $s \in S$ after action $a \in A$ has been executed.

The model of a POMDP consists of the transition model P_S, the observation model P_O, and the reward function r.

In a POMDP setting, the learning agent does not have access to the full state information $s_t \in S$. At every time $t \in T$, the agent makes an observation $o_t \in O$ of the current state s_t governed by a possibly stochastic observation model. The information provided by the observation o_t is merely a hint at state s_t, but does not completely reveal the state.

Since in subsequent chapters we will often refer to deterministic POMDPs, it is convenient to have a formal definition of deterministic POMDPs.

Definition 7. *Deterministic Partially Observable Markov Decision Process*
A deterministic partially observable Markov decision process
$M := (T, S, A, O, P_S, P_O, r)$ is a partially observable Markov decision process such that P_S can be represented by a deterministic transition function
$f_S : S \times A \to S$ and the stochastic observation model P_O can be represented by an observation function $f_O : A \times S \to O$. The function f_O gives for all actions $a \in A$ and all states $s \in S$ the observation $o \in O$, which is made after executing action a followed by a state transition to state s. A deterministic POMDP can be rewritten as $M := (T, S, A, O, f_S, f_O, r)$.

To illustrate the abstract state spaces generated by a POMDP, first consider the special case of a deterministic observation function $f_O : S \to O$ independent of actions. In such a setting, every observation $o \in O$ represents a region $z^o \subseteq S$ of the state space in which o is observed. Thus, observation o corresponds to an abstract state $z^o \subseteq S$. The complete abstract space Z is formed by the set of regions induced by the complete set of observations O. This special case of an unambiguous abstract state space is shown in Figure 3.2.

If the observation model is generalized to a function $f_O : A \times S \to O$, the same idea applies to a refined abstract state space $Z := \{z^{o_i, a_i} \mid 1 \leq i \leq 6\}$. An abstract state $z^{o,a} \in Z$ contains a state $s \in S$ if state s is reachable by action $a \in A$ and it holds that $f_O(a, s) = o$. Reachable means that there exists a state $s' \in S$ such that $f_S(s', a) = s$. Note that the resulting abstract state space is ambiguous, since some abstract states may overlap now. For example, if a state $s \in S$ is reachable by the two actions a_1, a_2 and it holds that $f_O(a_1, s) = o_1$ and $f_O(a_2, s) = o_1$, then state s is contained both by abstract state z^{o_1, a_1} as well as by abstract state z^{o_1, a_2}. However, it is still straightforward to define a policy $\pi : Z \to A$ on abstract states. The policy π selects action $\pi(z^{o,a})$ if observation o occurs after action a has been executed.

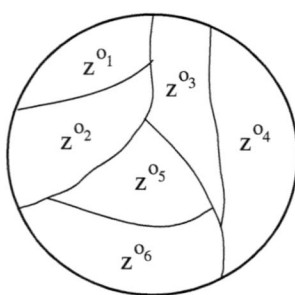

Figure 3.2: An abstract state space induced by an observation space. Each observation can be uniquely mapped to the subset of the state space in which the observation is made. The observation space consists of six distinct observations ($|O| = 6$). The resulting abstract state space is unambiguous.

The idea of generating abstract states by making observations can be even more generalized by considering sequences of observations and actions. For example, consider a sequence of past observations and actions $h := [a_0, o_1, a_1, ..., a_{t-1}, o_t]$. The abstract state z^h contains a state $s \in S$ if it is possible that s equals the current state s_t, given a certain history h of the process. This is exactly the sort of ambiguous abstract state space we will use for our algorithms presented in the next chapter. In Figure 3.3, an example of such an abstract state space is shown. The observation o_3 is made at all states within the outermost circle. Thus, the outermost circle represents an abstract state $z^{[o_3]}$ corresponding to a sequence containing only a single observation. However, by including information about events which happened before observation o_3 is made, two new abstract states $z^{[o_2, a_2, o_3]}$ and $z^{[o_1, a_1, o_2, a_2, o_3]}$ can be generated. These abstract states are subsets of the bigger abstract state $z^{[o_3]}$.

The abstract states shown in Figure 3.3 monotonically shrink with the length of the corresponding action-observation sequences. A long sequence corresponds to a small abstract state (small region of the state space), while a short sequence corresponds to a large abstract state (large region of the state space). In other words, by repeatedly extending sequences of past observations and actions, a relatively small set of states can be identified. The next chapter contains a detailed analysis concerning identifying sequences consisting of observations and actions.

Note that the abstract state space shown in Figure 3.3 is ambiguous, since the three abstract states are not disjoint. However, it is once again possible to define a policy on the created abstract state space. Such an approach is reasonable, since it can be shown that the optimal policy for a POMDP is defined on (possibly infinite) sequences of past observations and actions[1].

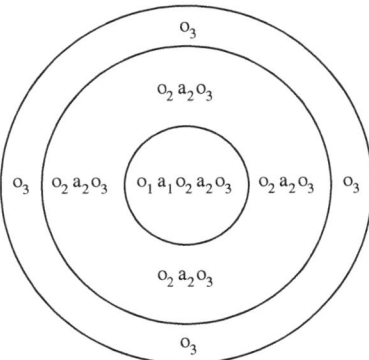

Figure 3.3: An abstract state space induced by sequences of observations and actions. The three circles correspond to the three abstract states $z^{[o_3]}$, $z^{[o_2,a_2,o_3]}$ and $z^{[o_1,a_1,o_2,a_2,o_3]}$. The outermost circle represents the region of the state space in which observation o_3 is made ($z^{[o_3]}$). The second, more inner circle represents the subset of states, in which the process may be after making observation o_2, then executing action a_2 and finally making observation o_3 ($z^{[o_2,a_2,o_3]}$). The innermost circle represents the subset of states in which the process may be after executing the actions a_1 and a_2 and making the observations o_1, o_2, and o_3 ($z^{[o_1,a_1,o_2,a_2,o_3]}$).

3.1.2 Discussion of Observation-Based Learning

We have shown that abstract state spaces can be created by observations of a partially observable Markov decision process (POMDP). However, the connection between abstract states and POMDPs is even stronger.

We assume that the original learning problem is given by an MDP. If the state space S is replaced by any kind of abstract state space Z, the underlying process changes from an MDP into a POMDP. This is due to the fact that abstract states are causing partial observability. If the learning agent processes

---
[1] In general, an optimal policy for a POMDP also depends on an initial belief state, i.e. a probability distribution over initial states. However, in all applications discussed in this work, the initial belief will be fixed.

solely abstract states, a large part of the original state information is pruned away.

However, most reinforcement learning algorithms dealing with abstract state spaces do not explicitly model abstract states by POMDPs. We therefore want to question the benefits of representing an abstract state space by a POMDP?

- The theoretical framework available for POMDPs is well-studied and there are many algorithms available for solving POMDPs. Thus, it is possible to reuse concepts and ideas from the literature. Prior work concerned with state abstractions often relies on heuristical assumptions, as discussed in the previous section. This is not the case for POMDPs. Most algorithms developed for POMDPs are sound in the sense that they converge to a unique policy. This policy can then be related to an optimal policy, which is, in the case of POMDPs, clearly defined. In general, all definitions and concepts in the context of POMDPs can be interpreted as straightforward extensions of single state spaces to abstract state spaces.

- A common technique for introducing state abstraction into reinforcement learning is to pre-process the current state by extracting a small number of features. These features be also interpreted as an observation of state and therefore constitute an abstract state space. Thus, the POMDP framework is compatible with a powerful tool for generating abstracting state spaces.

- In many practical problem settings, the state information processed by the learning agent can be regarded as an observation of state, since the sensory input is imprecise or incomplete. In such a situation, it is still possible to heuristically apply the standard methods available for MDPs. However, formulating those problems as POMDPs is much clearer from a conceptual point of view. If the state information is unreliable anyway, why not replace the original state space by features or other kinds of observations?

We will proceed with the following agenda:

1. Developing model-free algorithms for POMDPs.

2. Solving continuous problems by using POMDPs to represent an abstract state space.

A severe limitation of the standard algorithms for solving POMDPs is that the complete model is required in order to compute a policy. In the next chapter, we will present an algorithm able to overcome this limitation.

3.2 Optimal Policies for General POMDPs

In a POMDP setting, the only information available to the learning agent is the complete sequence of past observations and actions. Thus, the meaning of an optimal policy for a POMDP is significantly different compared to an optimal policy for an MDP. We will first review the basic definitions in the context of POMDPs and then derive the most important standard algorithm for solving POMDPs. Although the goal of this thesis is to develop model-free algorithms, the standard algorithms discussed in this chapter are model-based. This is due to the fact that there are no model-free algorithms available computing optimal policies for POMDPs. We will analyze the complexity of solving POMDPs and what concepts are needed for this purpose. It will turn out that even if a model is known in advance, every algorithm computing optimal policies for POMDPs is fundamentally inefficient. We will show that for deterministic POMDPs, near optimal policies can be learned also without a model.

The basic idea for solving a POMDP optimally is to transform it into an MDP by defining a Markovian process on an alternative state space, i.e. the information state space. The resulting MDP is therefore called the information state MDP and can be shown to be equivalent to the original POMDP. The value iteration procedure introduced in the last chapter can then be applied to the information state MDP in order to compute an optimal value function and an optimal policy.

Definition 8. *Information State*
Let $M := (T, S, A, O, P_S, P_O, r)$ be a partially observable Markov decision process. An information state I_t is defined to be the complete sequence of actions and observations $[a_0, o_1, a_1, o_2, ..., a_{t-1}, o_t]$ and a probability distribution over the initial state s_0 of the process[2]. The probability distribution represents a prior belief on the initial state.

The information state space I contains all possible information states, i.e. every possible prior belief on the initial state combined with all, possibly infinite sequences of observations and actions that can be generated by the transition model P_S and the observation model P_O.

To simplify notation, we will write $I_t := [a_0, o_1, ..., a_{t-1}, o_t]$ without explicitly stating the initial probability distribution over states. An information state summarizes all information the learning agent can use to estimate the current state $s_t \in S$. Since at time $t = 0$, there is no information available at all, the agent starts with a prior belief on the initial state $s_0 \in S$. At each of the following time steps $t > 0$, the information state is extended by the action executed and the most recent observation made.

The definition of the information state reflects the fact that in a POMDP setting, it is necessary to memorize past events in order to select an optimal action. The goal of a reinforcement learning agent is to take an optimal action based on all currently available information. Obviously, information states contain all such information. An optimal policy for a POMDP is therefore defined on the information state space.

---

[2] Note that if the observation model depends on the action executed, for example by a deterministic model $f_O : A \times S \to O$, then there exists no observation o_0 of the initial state s_0 of the process. It is easy to show that an observation model independent of actions can be formulated as a special case which need not to be treated separately.

Definition 9. *Policies for POMDPs*
Let $M := (T, S, A, O, P_S, P_O, r)$ be a partially observable Markov Decision Process. A policy for M is a set of mappings $\pi_I := \{\pi_t\}_{(t \in T)}$ such that each mapping $\pi_t : I \to A$ can be interpreted as a rule for choosing actions, given the current information state $I_t \in I$. Such a policy is called non-stationary, since the policy may change over time. If $\forall t \in T, \forall t' \in T : \pi_t = \pi_{t'}$, then the set of mappings reduces to a single stationary policy $\pi_I : I \to A$.

The set Π_I denotes the space of all possible policies on information states, including both non-stationary policies as well as stationary ones.

Definition 10. *Optimal Policies for POMDPs*
Let $M := (T, S, A, O, P_S, P_O, r)$ be a partially observable Markov decision process and let $0 \leq \beta \leq 1$ be a discounting factor. If the set of time steps T is finite such that $T_F \in T$ is the maximal element of T, then a policy $\pi_I^* := \{\pi_t\}_{(t \in T)}$ is called optimal with respect to M if it holds that
$\pi_I^* \in \arg\max_{\pi_I \in \Pi_I} E_{\{I_t, s_t\}}[\sum_{t=0}^{T_F-1} \beta^t r(s_t, \pi_t(I_t)) + \beta^{T_F} r(s_{T_F}, \cdot)]$.

If the set of time steps T is infinite, then a policy $\pi_I^* := \{\pi_t\}_{(t \in T)}$ is called optimal if it holds that $\pi_I^* \in \arg\max_{\pi_I \in \Pi_I} E_{\{I_t, s_t\}}[\sum_{t=0}^{\infty} \beta^t r(s_t, \pi_t(I_t))]$.

We will now specify the transformation of a POMDP into an information state MDP. As we will show by Lemma 3, the information state MDP and the original POMDP are equivalent. Thus, it is sufficient to compute an optimal policy for the information state MDP. This policy is also optimal for the original POMDP.

Definition 11. *Information State MDP*
Let $M := (T, S, A, O, P_S, P_O, r)$ be a partially observable Markov decision process. The information state MDP is given by a five-tuple $M_I := (T, I, A, P_I, r_I)$. A stochastic transition from an information state $I_t = \{a_0, o_1, ..., a_{t-1}, o_t\}$ to a next information state $I_{t+1} = \{a_0, o_1, ..., a_{t-1}, o_t, a_t = a, o_{t+1} = o\}$ occurs with probability $P_I(I_{t+1} \mid I_t, a) := p(o \mid I_t, a)$. The term $p(o \mid I_t, a)$ denotes the probability of making the observation $o \in O$ after executing action $a \in A$, given the information state I_t.

The reward function r_I is defined as $r_I(I_t, a_t) := \sum_{s \in S} p(s_t = s \mid I_t) r(s, a_t)$. The term $p(s_t = s \mid I_t)$ denotes the probability that the current state $s_t \in S$ equals $s \in S$, given the information state I_t.

It remains to show that the information state MDP actually exists, i.e. the model of M_I is well-defined and M_I constitutes a valid MDP.

Lemma 2. *Existence of the Information State MDP*
Let $M := (T, S, A, O, P_S, P_O, r)$ be a partially observable Markov decision process. The information state MDP $M_I := (T, I, A, P_I, r_I)$ satisfies the Markov assumption and the model of M_I is well-defined.

Lemma 3. *Equivalence of POMDP and Information State MDP*
Let $M := (T, S, A, O, P_S, P_O, r)$ be a partially observable Markov decision process and let $M_I := (T, I, A, P_I, r_I)$ be the corresponding information state MDP. Then, it holds that

$$\pi_I^* \text{ is optimal for } M_I \Leftrightarrow \pi_I^* \text{ is optimal for } M$$

The proofs for Lemma 2 and Lemma 3 can be found in the appendix. The transformation of a POMDP M into an information state MDP M_I is especially useful, because in the last chapter we derived a model-based algorithm for solving MDPs. If the model of M_I is known, the value iteration algorithm (Equation (2.2)) can be used to compute an optimal policy for M_I. Since Lemma 3 guarantees that an optimal policy for M_I is also optimal for M, such a procedure will yield an optimal solution for M.

For the special case of an information state MDP, the system of Bellman equations used by the value iteration algorithm takes on the following form:

$$V_n^* : I \to \mathbb{R}, \; V_n^*(I') = \max_{a \in A}[r_I(I', a) + \beta \sum_{I'' \in I} P_I(I'' \mid I', a) V_{n+1}^*(I'')] \quad (3.1)$$

As for the fully observable case considered in the last chapter, the parameter n takes on values from the interval $[0, T_F - 1]$. The initial value function $V_{T_F}^*$ is given by $V_{T_F}^*(I') = r_I(I', \cdot)$. If we reinsert the definitions of P_I and r_I into Equation (3.1), we can rewrite the Bellman equation in a slightly different, but more explicit form.

$$V_n^*(I_t) = \max_{a \in A}[\sum_{s \in S} p(s_t = s \mid I_t) r(s, a)$$
$$+ \beta \sum_{o \in O} p(o_{t+1} = o \mid I_t, a) V_{n+1}^*(I_{t+1} = \{a_0, o_1, ..., a_t = a, o_{t+1} = o\})]$$
$$(3.2)$$

Starting with a fixed initial belief I_0, i.e. a probability distribution over the initial state $s_0 \in S$, the values of all information states $I' \in I$ are implicitly given by Equation (3.2). Keeping the initial belief fixed is necessary to ensure that the information state space remains countable. Thus, Lemma 1 for proving optimality of the value iteration procedure still applies.

Unfortunately, there is no practical procedure for actually computing these values. This is due to the fact that the information state space I contains infinitely many information states and it is therefore intractable to iterate over Equation (3.2). Moreover, an information state itself is possibly of infinite length. Thus, it is not clear how to apply the value iteration algorithm in such a setting. To obtain a practical version of value iteration, it is necessary to derive a compact representation for information states as well as for value functions V_n^*.

3.2.1 Belief States and Piecewise Linear Value Functions

An information state explicitly enumerates every piece of information the learning agent receives from the environment, i.e. the complete sequence of observations resulting from the sequence of actions executed. Since the complete sequence of observations and actions is possibly of infinite size, it is favorable to compress this sequence somehow.

The key idea to achieve such a compression is that information states are equivalent to probability distributions over states[3]. These distributions are called belief states, since they express the belief of the learning agent about the current state of the process.

Definition 12. *Belief States*
The belief state b_t at time t is an $|S|$-dimensional vector such that every component corresponds to the probability of a certain state $s \in S$. The components of b_t are defined as $b_t(s) := p(s_t = s \mid I_t)$ and therefore form a probability distribution over states.

For the special case $t = 0$, it holds that $b_0 = I_0$, since I_0 is the prior belief, i.e. a probability distribution over the initial state $s_0 \in S$. The benefit of belief states compared to information states is that a belief state is a vector of finite size, while an information state is a possibly infinite sequence.

To prove that the concept of information states is equivalent to the concept of belief states, it is necessary to express the value functions from Equation (3.2) in terms of belief states. Given such a result, it would be possible to apply value iteration using belief states instead of information states.

Theorem 2. *Belief States Form a Sufficient Statistic*
Let $M := (T, S, A, O, P_S, P_O, r)$ be a partially observable Markov decision process and let $M_I := (T, I, A, P_I, r_I)$ be the corresponding information state MDP. If the set of time steps T is finite such that T_F is a maximal element of T, then it is possible to rewrite the optimal value functions V_n^* ($0 \leq n \leq T_F$) in terms of belief states.

$$V_n^*(b) := \max_{a \in A} [\sum_{s \in S} b(s) r(s,a) + \beta \sum_{o \in O} \sum_{s' \in S, s'' \in S} P_O(o \mid s'', a) \cdot P_S(s'' \mid s', a) b(s') V_{n+1}^*(b_o^a)] \quad (3.3)$$

The belief state b_o^a denotes the successor belief of b after executing action $a \in A$ and making observation $o \in O$.

$$b_o^a(s) := \frac{P_O(o \mid s, a) \sum_{s' \in S} P_S(s \mid s', a) b(s')}{\sum_{s' \in S, s'' \in S} P_S(s'' \mid s', a) P_O(o \mid s'', a) b(s')} \quad (3.4)$$

The initial value function $V_{T_F}^*$ is given by the expected terminal reward at time T_F.

$$V_{T_F}^*(b) := \sum_{s \in S} b(s) r(s, \cdot) \quad (3.5)$$

---

[3] An early proof of this well known result is given, for example, in [SS73].

The proof of Theorem 2 can be found in the appendix. Equation (3.3) enables us to compute the sequence of optimal value functions solely based on the model of the original POMDP. Since a belief state is a vector of finite size, an update of the value function for a single belief state can be easily computed by summing over the state space and the observation space. Here, updating the value function at a belief state b means to compute the value function $V_n^*(b)$ at belief state b from Equation (3.3).

Since there are still infinitely many belief states, it remains impractical to perform value iteration updates on all those states. This is easy to see since the space of probability distributions (belief space) is an uncountable set. A solution to this problem was presented in [SS73] by showing that a value function defined on belief states is piecewise linear and convex. Moreover, this value function can be represented by a set of vectors.

Definition 13. *Convex Polytopes*
A set $M \subseteq \mathbb{R}^n$ is called a convex polytope, if there exists a finite set of vertices $V \subset \mathbb{R}^n$ such that M equals the convex hull of V. The convex hull of a finite set of vertices $V := \{v_1, ..., v_k\}$ is given by all linear combinations of the form $\lambda_1 v_1 + \lambda_2 v_2 + ... + \lambda_n v_k$ satisfying $\sum_{i=1}^{k} \lambda_i = 1$ and $\lambda_i \geq 0$ ($1 \leq i \leq k$).

It is easy to show that convex polyptopes are actually convex sets.

Definition 14. *Piecewise Linear Functions*
A function $f : M \to \mathbb{R}$ with $M \subseteq \mathbb{R}^n$ is called piecewise linear, if the set M can be partitioned into a finite set of convex polytopes such that f is linear on each of these polytopes.

Definition 15. *Convex Functions*
A function $f : M \to \mathbb{R}$ with $M \subset \mathbb{R}^n$ is called convex, if the following condition is satisfied for every $x \in M, y \in M$ and $0 \leq \lambda \leq 1$:

$$f(\lambda x + (1 - \lambda)y) \leq \lambda f(x) + (1 - \lambda)f(y)$$

The sequence of optimal value functions V_n^* ($0 \leq n \leq T_F$) can be computed by repeatedly building a set of vectors Γ_n from an already computed set of vectors Γ_{n+1}. By such a procedure, it is not necessary to explicitly perform value iteration updates on single belief states. The next theorem provides the instructions necessary to build the sets of vectors Γ_n and the value functions V_n^*, respectively.

Theorem 3. *Compact Representation of the Value Function*
Let $M := (T, S, A, O, P_S, P_O, r)$ be a partially observable Markov decision process. If the set of time steps T is finite such that $T_F \in T$ is a maximal element of T, then the optimal value functions V_n^* ($0 \leq t \leq T_F$) with respect to M are piecewise linear and convex. Moreover, V_n^* can be represented by a finite set of vectors Γ_n such that $V_n^*(b) = \max_{\gamma \in \Gamma_n} b * \gamma$. The $*$ symbol denotes the dot product of two vectors. The set Γ_{T_F} consists of the single vector $R(s) := r(s, \cdot)$.

For $0 \leq n < T_F$, it holds that

$$\Gamma_n := \{\sum_{o \in O} \alpha_{f(o)}^{o,a} \mid f \in f(O, \Gamma_{n+1}),\ a \in A\}$$

$$\forall \gamma \in \Gamma_{n+1}: \alpha_\gamma^{o,a}(s') := \frac{r(s',a)}{|O|} + \beta \sum_{s \in S} P_O(o \mid s, a) P_S(s \mid s', a) \gamma(s)$$

The symbol $f(O, \Gamma_{n+1})$ denotes the set of possible mappings from observations to vectors from Γ_{n+1}.

The proof of Theorem 3 can be found in the appendix. The piecewise linear value function of a POMDP can be imagined as dividing the belief space into regions. These regions consists of convex polytopes on which the value function is linear. Every vector $\gamma \in \Gamma_n$ corresponds to a certain region such that γ maximizes the dot product $\gamma * b$ for all belief states b within this region. Thus, the number of regions forming the complete value function V_n^* is equivalent to the number of vectors in Γ_n.

However, if the horizon is infinite, i.e. there is no maximal element $T_F \in T$, there may be infinitely many regions such that the value function cannot be represented by a finite set of vectors. Thus, the optimal value function is not necessarily piecewise linear for general POMDPs. Although there are algorithms tackling the infinite horizon problem [Son78], the analysis of these algorithms is out of the scope of this thesis. For the rest of the thesis, we rely on the assumption that an infinite horizon POMDP can be approximated sufficiently well by a POMDP with a very large, but finite horizon.

3.2.2 Analysis of Exact Value Iteration for POMDPs

The standard algorithm for model-based solving POMDPs is the value iteration procedure. A naive implementation of the value iteration procedure is given by Algorithm 2. The same notation is used as for Theorem 3.

Algorithm 2 Value Iteration for POMDPs

1: $n \leftarrow T_F$
2: $\forall s \in S: \gamma(s) \leftarrow \max_{a \in A} r(s,a),\ \Gamma_n \leftarrow \{\gamma\}$
3: **repeat**
4: $\quad n \leftarrow n - 1$
5: $\quad \forall o \in O, \forall a \in A, \forall \gamma \in \Gamma_{n+1}, \forall s' \in S:$
$\quad \alpha_\gamma^{o,a}(s') \leftarrow \frac{r(s',a)}{|O|} + \beta \sum_{s \in S} P_O(o \mid s, a) P_S(s \mid s', a) \gamma(s)$
6: $\quad \Gamma_n \leftarrow \{\sum_{o \in O} \alpha_{f(o)}^{o,a} \mid f \in f(O, \Gamma_{n+1}),\ a \in A\}$
7: **until** $[n = 0]$

We want to analyze how much time is consumed by a single iteration of the main loop. Creating the α-vectors is quadratic in $|S|$ and linear in $|A|, |O|, |\Gamma_{n+1}|$. The computation of the set Γ_n is linear in $|O|, |A|$ and $|f(O, \Gamma_{n+1})|$. Since

$f(O, \Gamma_{n+1})$ is the set of mappings from observations to vectors from Γ_{n+1}, it holds that $|f(O, \Gamma_{n+1})| = |\Gamma_{n+1}|^{|O|}$. Thus, the set of vectors needed to represent the value functions grows exponentially in the size of the observations space. After only a few iterations of the loop, the set Γ_n may become intractably large. This is the reason why the standard form of value iteration for POMDPs is not applicable for all but the smallest problems.

A simple idea for tuning the algorithm is to prune away all redundant vectors from Γ_n after every iteration of the loop. It may be the case that a subset $\Gamma_n^* \subset \Gamma_n$ of vectors is already sufficient to represent the value function V_n^*. A vector $\gamma \in \Gamma_n$ is called redundant if there is no belief state b such that the dot product $b * \gamma$ is maximal with respect the complete set of vectors Γ_n. Since it holds that $V_n^*(b) = \max_{\gamma \in \Gamma_n} b * \gamma$, it is easy to prove that only non-redundant vectors from Γ_n are necessary to represent V_n^*.

Although some research is available about finding clever pruning strategies, it is not guaranteed that Γ_n actually contains redundant vectors. In the worst case, all vectors from the set Γ_n are necessary to represent the value function V_n^*. Examples for such worst cases may be found in [LCK95]. To summarize, computing optimal policies for POMDPs by the value iteration procedure is fundamentally inefficient. Even for deterministic POMDPs, it is possible to prove that finding an optimal policy is NP-hard [Lit94].

3.2.3 Alternatives to the Value Iteration Algorithm

Almost every model-based algorithm for solving POMDPs is based on the value iteration algorithm or at least shares some of the key ideas with this algorithm. We will now give a short overview of the different approaches for modifying or extending value iteration. Except for the algorithms from the field of policy search, all algorithms discussed will still be model-based.

Exact Algorithms

Solving a POMDP exactly means performing full backups of the value function as shown in Algorithm 2. Possible extensions of the value iteration algorithm narrow down to clever strategies for computing a sufficiently large subset $\Gamma_n^* \subset \Gamma_n$ containing less redundant vectors. However, in the worst case, all of these approaches take time exponentially in the size of the observation space.

One of the first exact algorithms is the one-pass algorithm presented in [SS73]. Starting with an abitrary belief b, the maximal vector γ_b for b is computed and added to Γ_n. Next, the region of the belief space is computed, in which γ_b is maximal. By inspecting the boundaries of this region, all neighboring regions and their corresponding maximal vectors are identified. The process is iterated until all regions of the belief space are covered.

The linear support algorithm [Che88] concentrates on finding corners (vertices) of the regions partitioning the belief space. The algorithm exploits the fact that every region must have corners, since the regions consist of convex polytopes. If for every region of the belief space at least one corner is found, all non-redundant vectors from Γ_n can be computed.

The goal of the witness algorithm from [LCK95] is again to avoid computing too many redundant vectors from Γ_n. The algorithm makes use of the fact that it is possible to define a neighborhood of a vector from Γ_n. In order to find new vectors from Γ_n, only the neighborhoods of already found vectors must be searched. The algorithm terminates if all identified neighborhoods contain only redundant vectors.

A clever strategy for pruning vectors from Γ_n is presented in [CLZ97]. The basic idea is to interleave the computation of the set Γ_n with pruning steps to remove redundant vectors. By using such a procedure, it is likely (but not guaranteed) that the size of Γ_n remains relatively small.

Point-Based Algorithms

Since computing optimal solutions for POMDPs is proven to be intractable, it is reasonable to ask if it is possible to approximate the optimal policy. The basic idea of point-based algorithms is to concentrate the value iteration backups on a finite set of belief states.

A first step in this direction was made in [ZZ01] by interleaving full backups as shown in Algorithm 2 with point-based backups on single beliefs, as shown in Equation (3.3). By implementing such a procedure, it is possible to speed up the computation of the new vector set Γ_n. However, the algorithm still computes the optimal value function and therefore shares the drawbacks of the exact approaches.

Best known for point-based value iteration backups is the PBVI algorithm from [PGT03]. In PBVI, a fixed set of belief states B is considered. Every belief in B corresponds to a single vector $\gamma \in \Gamma_n$ used to represent the value function. The benefit of point-based methods is that the size of Γ_n is fixed and does not exceed the size of B. The modified value iteration procedure concentrates the backups solely on the finite set B of belief states. The computed value function is suboptimal, but can be related somehow to the optimal value function. Several heuristics for including additional belief states to B are discussed in order to increase the accuracy of the value function approximation. A similar idea to PBVI is the Perseus algorithm, presented in [SV05]. Again, the set of vectors used to represent the value function is of fixed size. The authors argue that Perseus is a practical method, which can be used even for continuous action spaces.

An alternative to point-based backups (Equation (3.3)) are grid-based backups. A grid consists of a finite set of belief states spread over the entire belief space. The value function for an arbitrary belief is approximated by a linear combination of values from the grid. The grids used can either be regular or irregular. In a regular grid, the distance between two neighboring grid points is fixed. In [Bra97], the first grid-based approach was presented. Although the procedure for computing the coefficients of the linear combinations is a heuristic, the algorithm performed very well on benchmark problems. In [Hau00], several other grid-based approaches are analyzed and discussed. An important theoretical result concerning grids is presented in [Hau00]: If the linear combinations used to approximate the value function are convex, the resulting approximation is an upper bound of the optimal value function.

Finite State Automata

If the value function can be represented by a finite set of vectors, it is straightforward to show that a greedy policy extracted from the value function can also be represented by a finite state automaton (FSA). The nodes of such an automaton correspond to the vectors from Γ_n and the edges correspond to local policies defined on observations. A simple idea for computing policies for POMDPs is therefore to search in the space of FSAs.

In [Han98], value iteration backups are used to refine a policy given as an FSA. The value iteration procedure is interleaved with a heuristic search in order to modify the current FSA found. The problem with FSAs is that the number of nodes can grow rapidly after a few steps of value iteration. This is due to the fact that the nodes of the FSA exactly correspond to the vectors from Γ_n. In [PB04], this problem is tackled by introducing stochastic policies for FSAs. Each node of the FSA is optimized by improving its local stochastic policy. This is accomplished by a linear program. If a local optimum is reached, i.e. no node can be further improved, it is either possible to escape from the local optimum or add additional nodes to the automaton.

In [MKKC99], two distinct search procedures for finding FSAs with good performance are presented. The first approach is a branch and bound search in the space of deterministic FSAs. The bounds are computed by solving a system of Bellman equations very similar to the equations used for the value iteration algorithm. The second approach performs gradient ascent in the space of stochastic FSAs. A set of parameters for a stochastic policy is defined, consisting of the transition probabilities to other nodes and the probabilities of taking a certain action in a node. The value function of a policy can then be stated in terms of the parameters. An update of the current policy is performed by computing the derivatives of the value function with respect to the parameters and shifting the parameters to a higher expected cumulative reward. More search heuristics for finding good stochastic FSAs are presented in [BB04].

Chapter 4

Solving POMDPs without a Model

A problem formulated as a POMDP can be solved optimally using the methods described in the previous chapter only if enough prior knowledge is available. To perform value iteration steps, either exactly or approximatively, it is necessary to know the model of the POMDP, i.e. the transition probabilities P_S, the observation model P_O and the reward function r. Even if all this information is given in advance, solving POMDPs remains a very difficult problem. There is provably no efficient model-based algorithm computing optimal solutions [LCK95].

This chapter addresses the problem of solving POMDPs without a model. It is reasonable to ask if it is possible to circumvent some of the fundamental problems model-based algorithms have. In particular, we want to question the concept of optimality in a classical POMDP setting. Learning an optimal policy for a POMDP means finding an optimal action for every possible probability distribution over states. In order to achieve this, the belief space concept is employed, substituting the original state space of the process. However, for many reinforcement learning problems, such a representation of a state is impractical. For the following reasons, we think that model-free methods, i.e. methods given no prior knowledge about the model, should avoid a belief state representation.

- Belief states are only practical for small, finite state spaces, since a belief state is a vector of size $|S|$. The belief space, i.e. all possible belief states, is an uncountable set even for small state spaces.

- Updating the values of a belief state requires a model (Equation (3.3)) which is not available in a model-free setting. Learning the transition model P_S from data, for example by an approach from stochastic approximation, is very hard since the learning agent is never certain about the current state. Moreover, it would be necessary to learn the observation model P_O, as well.

- Since the model of a POMDP constitutes prior knowledge about the learning problem, solving a problem without the model is much more challenging than solving a problem model-based. Even if a model is available, there is no efficient algorithm for computing optimal policies on belief states. Finding optimal policies on belief states seems therefore to be an intractable problem in general.

To find alternatives for the belief state concept, it is instructive to once more discuss the very basic ideas for solving POMDPs. Since a POMDP is a Markov process, an optimal policy can be computed solely based on the current state of the process [BT96]. However, the only information available in a POMDP setting to infer the current state is the complete sequence of past observations and actions. This sequence is called the information state. In order to keep track of the information state, the learning agent has to use some form of memory. A belief state is perfect memory in the sense that it incorporates every past event without ever forgetting a single piece of information. This is reflected by the fact, that belief states and information states are equivalent concepts (Theorem 2).

Unfortunately, as discussed above, perfect memory in the form of belief states or information states is not well-suited for efficient algorithms. We therefore propose that the learning agent memorizes an approximation of the information state instead of the complete information state. A policy executed by the learning agent can be defined on this approximated information state.

We will now present various types of memory proven to be useful for approximatively solving POMDPs. We will concentrate solely on model-free methods, which are, in some cases, extensions of model-based methods already discussed in the last chapter.

4.1 Different Types of Memory

4.1.1 Without Memory

A simple form of estimating the current state is to ignore all past events and search for policies $\pi : O \to A$ defined on the most recent observation made. Such memoryless policies seem to make the problem much simpler. Surprisingly, this is not the case. In [Lit94], it is shown that even for deterministic POMDPs learning the best memoryless policy without a model is NP-hard. Thus, in [Lit94] a branch and bound heuristic is proposed to find the best memoryless policy. The algorithm always finds the best policy, but possibly tries all ($|A|^{|O|}$) policies in the worst case.

More theoretical results concerning memoryless policies are provided by Singh et. al. [SJJ94]. They show that even if only a small fraction of the state space is partially observable, the best memoryless policy can be arbitrarily poor compared to the optimal solution. Moreover, they showed that the best stochastic memoryless policy can be arbitrarily better than the best deterministic memoryless policy. This result inspired many of the numerous approaches for learning stochastic policies. Note, however, that in the fully observable case (MDP), there is always an optimal deterministic policy. A related article [JSJ94] presents an algorithm for learning stochastic memoryless policies trying to maximize the average reward gained per step. The algorithm is not guaranteed to find the best stochastic policy, but can be shown to converge to a local maximum[1].

A very popular heuristic for solving POMDPs with stochastic, memoryless policies is gradient descent. In [IM98], the Vaps algorithm is introduced, which assumes a stochastic policy to be parametrized by a parameter vector θ. By estimating the gradient on some error function with respect to the vector θ, the parameters can be updated in order to minimize the errors made. As a reasonable error measure, they propose the Bellman residual emerging as a result of Q-learning updates (or other typical forms of updates, e.g. Sarsa). The Bellman residual is given by the quadratic difference of a Q-factor $Q(s, a)$ before and after a Q-learning update for this Q-factor. The authors claim that the algorithm can be applied both to MDPs and POMDPs. A well known extension of Vaps is given in [PMK99]. Instead of using the Bellman residual, the negative discounted sum of rewards is used as an error measure. Thus, minimizing the error corresponds to maximizing the discounted cumulative reward. In contrast to Vaps, the algorithm uses memory by augmenting the observation space by a single bit. This bit can be set/reset by special actions added to the action space. The learning agent can make use of memory by setting and resetting the bit.

There are a lot of other algorithms using gradient descent to learn stochastic, memoryless policies, which we will not discuss in detail, for example in [Wil92], [SMSM99], [PVS05]. The major problem with gradient descent is the existence of local minima, which can trap the learning process at an early stage. Moreover, the quality of the learned policies heavily depends on the kind of parametrization used. For finding a good initial setting of parameters, it is necessary to have some prior knowledge about the problem.

In the context of this thesis, algorithms related to learning memoryless policies can be primarily found in [BG98], [LR02] and [TR05]. The goal of these model-free approaches is to find a policy by a heuristic search based on a set of observations of the current state. The search algorithms are efficient variants of classical search methods such as backtracking. Although good policies can be found very quickly for some tasks, the theoretical guarantees concerning convergence issues and the quality of the learned policies are rather weak. In the worst case, all possible policies must be enumerated causing the search procedures to have exponential complexity. Thus, the methods may not scale well to complex tasks.

The last approach for learning memoryless policies we want to discuss is eligibility traces. Loch and Singh [LS98] yielded surprisingly good results by applying Sarsa(λ) to a set of benchmark (POMDP) problems. The reason for

---

[1] The notion of a local maximum used in [JSJ94] is somewhat different from the common meaning of this term. See [JSJ94] for details.

the success of Sarsa(λ) is that for high values of λ (e.g. $\lambda \approx 1$), the Sarsa(λ) algorithm is very similar to a Monte Carlo stochastic approximation method. Such methods do not rely on the Markov assumption, as is the case for traditional Q-learning. Since the Markov assumption is violated if a policy is defined on observations, Q-learning will fail to converge to an optimal policy. Although the Sarsa(λ) algorithm yields better empirical results than Q-learning in a POMDP setting, it is not guaranteed to converge to an optimal policy, as well.

4.1.2 History Lists and Suffix Trees

A still very simple form of memory is maintaining a finite list of past observations and actions. Such a list constitutes a suffix of the complete, possibly infinite list of actually emerged observations and actions. A memory based on history lists will therefore forget past events after a finite horizon of time. History approaches always implement short-term memory. Due to the simplicity and the clarity of the list concept, history lists are one of the most practical state representations for POMDPs. We will give a formal definition of a history list in the next section, but we first want to sketch the most important previous work. A set of history lists is often represented as a suffix tree, such that every branch of the tree corresponds to a single history list (Figure 4.1).

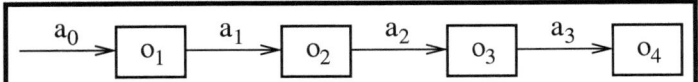

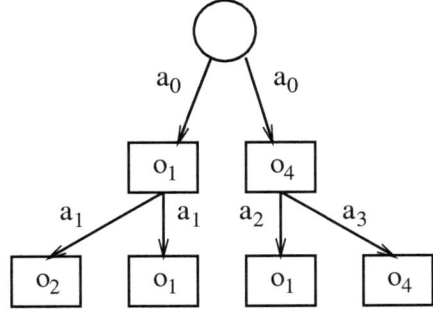

Figure 4.1: History lists and suffix trees. A history list consists of a single sequence of observations and actions, while a tree possibly contains several such sequences. For example, the leftmost branch of the tree shown in the figure is a prefix of the history list above.

In [McC94], the current state s_t is represented by the complete sequence of past observations and actions that occurred on the currently sampled episode. To compute a Q-value for the current state s_t and action a_t, first a measure of similarity (neighborhood) is computed with respect to all states $s_{t'}$ at previous time steps $t' < t$ with $a_{t'} = a_t$. The similarity of the current state to another state depends on the longest suffix of past observations and actions shared by the two states. If a state shares a long suffix of equal experience with the current state, it is considered to be similar to the current state. The Q-value of the current state is then computed by building an average value over the Q-values of similar states, weighted by their degree of similarity. Then, all states involved in the computation of the Q-value are updated according to a rule similar to traditional Q-learning. There is no guarantee that this procedure will find an optimal policy nor that the Q-values will converge to a fixed point. The algorithm relies on the heuristical assumption that all actually occurring states can be distinguished by looking at their history of observations and actions.

The most popular model-free algorithm on history lists is the U-tree algorithm developed in [McC95]. Here, history lists are contained in a suffix tree of finite depth, which again distinguishes sequences of past observations and actions. The states of the POMDP are represented by the leaves of the tree. A transition instance $o_t \rightarrow o_{t+1}$ collected on a sampled episode is classified by the suffix tree and is then assigned to a leave representing a state. A model for a state is built by counting the frequency of transitions to other states. Value iteration steps can be performed on the approximate model yielding a policy. To refine the state space after sampling a number of transition instances, a leave is expanded and new leaves are created below the old leave. If the Q-values of the new leaves are not significantly different compared to the old one, the splitting of the old leave is revoked. Significance is detected by using the Kolmogorov-Smirnov Test [Bos98]. Since a Q-function gives the expected cumulative reward, the method used to split a leave can be regarded as reward-based. Again, the procedure is not guaranteed to converge to a unique Q-function.

Interestingly, the U-tree algorithm does not aim at perfectly reestablishing the original state space of the underlying POMDP. The states are created solely based on their importance for increasing the cumulative reward. Thus, it will not be possible to uniquely identify every state of the POMDP. This is desirable in a sense, since the procedure is able to generalize over states. On the other hand, if some states are indistinguishable, this will destroy all desirable properties of the value iteration algorithm (e.g. convergence issues). It is not possible to relate the quality of the policy found to the optimal solution on belief states, since U-tree uses many heuristics that are hard to analyze.

A more recent algorithm for model-free learning of suffix trees in the context of partially observable environments is given in [HJ06]. The algorithm is restricted to deterministic environments, ignores reward signals and does not compute any policies. The leaves of the tree again correspond to states of the POMDP. In contrast to U-tree, a tree is learned able to predict future observations instead of future rewards. Under certain assumptions, it can be shown that the algorithm can resolve any disambiguities between states. A special feature of this algorithm is that the learned tree possibly contains loops. This enables dealing with long subsequences of useless information, which can be sandwiched in an enclosing sequence. We will discuss some important aspects of this algorithm later in more detail.

4.1.3 Stochastic Finite State Controller

A stochastic finite state controller consists of a finite number of nodes connected by a directed graph. Each edge of this graph corresponds to the probability of a transition from one node to another, given the most recent observation made. Additionally, a probability distribution over actions is given for each state, representing a local stochastic policy. Thus, a stochastic finite state controller constitutes a stochastic memory-based policy for POMDPs.

It can be shown that finite state controllers are able approximate the optimal policy on belief states arbitrarily well ([Son78], [KLC96]). For a certain class of POMDPs (finitely transient), it is possible to prove that there always exists a deterministic finite state controller equivalent to the optimal policy [Son78]. Despite the impressive theoretical properties of finite state controllers, there is

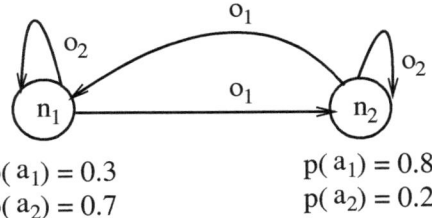

Figure 4.2: Stochastic finite state controller. The figure shows a stochastic finite state controller with two nodes and two actions. In this example, the local policies are stochastic, while the state transitions are deterministic.

not much work available for learning these controllers without a model. We will discuss only the best known approach given in [MPKK99], which is an extension of a model-based method [MKKC99] already discussed in the previous chapter. In [MPKK99], the transition probabilities and the stochastic local policies are parametrized using a set of weights $\{w_k\}$. The controller is fully specified by these probability distributions. Similar to the extension of the Vaps algorithm in [PMK99], an expression for the expected cumulative reward of such a parametrized policy is derived. It is now possible to compute the gradient of this expression with respect to the weight vector and to shift the weight vector in the direction of higher rewards. Like all approaches using gradient ascent, the algorithm finds a local maximum instead of the global maximum. Moreover, it is not possible to relate the controller found to the optimal controller. In contrast to the model-based algorithms for finite state controllers, this algorithm can be regarded as a heuristic. Until now, it is not clear how optimal finite state controllers can be learned efficiently without any information about the model.

4.1.4 Recurrent Neural Networks

Artificial neural networks have been successfully applied to reinforcement learning problems in the past, for example in [Tes94]. They can either be used as a function approximator to represent the Q-function or to represent a policy directly. A recurrent neural network is a network with cyclic connections of neurons as shown in Figure 4.3. Since the output of the network at time step t is fed back to the input neurons at the next time step $t+1$, recurrent networks do implement some form of memory. Thus, recurrent networks are potentially useful for solving POMDPs. Note that Figure 4.3 represents only one possible architecture for recurrent neural networks. In fact, there are many different architectures available, which will not be discussed in this thesis. To adapt the weights of each neuron, several algorithms can be used, all having their roots in gradient descent. Best known are Backpropagation Through Time [Pea89] and Real Time Recurrent Learning [RF87].

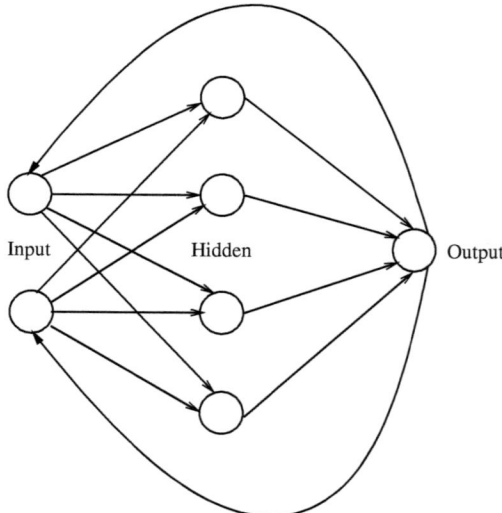

Figure 4.3: A recurrent neural network. The figure shows a network with two input units, four hidden units and one output unit.

In [LM92], feed-forward networks are compared to several architectures of recurrent neural networks with respect to their ability to solve POMDPs. It is shown that in contrast to feed-forward networks, recurrent networks are able to make use of memory and therefore solve reinforcement learning problems with partial observability. In particular, two architectures of recurrent networks are distinguished.

1. A single recurrent network, which is used to approximate a Q-function.
2. A combination of two recurrent networks. While the first network estimates the model of the POMDP, the second network approximates a value function. The second network is trained by using the approximate model from the first network.

Since the standard algorithms used to train recurrent neural networks can be applied to a wide range of network topologies, there are many other architectures of neural networks available, all specialized for certain tasks. A well known architecture for recurrent neural networks, especially applicable to POMDPs is Long Short-Term Memory [Bak01]. Again, a Q-function is approximated by a recurrent network consisting of different types of neurons. In addition to memory neurons for storing the incoming input, there are special neurons available called gates. The gates control the information flow generated by the input/output units. What makes gates especially interesting is that they enable the memory cells to forget some pieces of information stored. This corresponds to the idea of establishing an approximated information state as discussed above.

To directly represent a policy by a recurrent neural network, mostly evolutionary techniques are employed. In [GS05], both the topology of the network as well as the weights of individual neurons are evolved. Empirical results show that evolutionary approaches are able to solve typical POMDP problem settings. A principal problem of evolutionary methods is that the search over networks can be trapped in local minima, preventing the search to find the optimal network.

Similar to history lists, recurrent neural networks are a very practical approach for solving POMDPs. Recurrent neural networks can deal with multi-dimensional observation spaces as well as with multi-dimensional action spaces. However, there is only little theory available on reinforcement learning with recurrent neural networks. It is not yet clearly understood how recurrent neural networks process the information stored in memory and what the limitations of such an approach are. Again, it is not possible to relate the learned policy to the optimal solution on belief states.

4.1.5 Hidden Markov Models

Hidden Markov models (HMMs) and partially observable Markov decision processes (POMDPs) are closely related, since every POMDP also contains an HMM. Stated precisely, the transition model and the observation model of a POMDP constitute an HMM. On the contrary, an HMM does not contain a POMDP, since an HMM ignores reward signals. The form of memory used in HMMs is equivalent to the belief space formulation for POMDPs and therefore shares all drawbacks of this representation. However, the problem setting in an HMM is fundamentally different from the problem setting in a POMDP. While typical HMM algorithms try to learn the unknown model from data, a learning algorithm for POMDPs aims at maximizing the discounted cumulative reward. A direct way of employing HMM techniques for solving POMDPs is to first to learn a model of the POMDP (e.g. with the Baum-Welch algorithm [BPSW70]) and then perform exact value iteration updates on belief states as described in the last chapter. Unfortunately, as already discussed, there are no efficient algorithms available for computing the optimal value function.

Another problem is that estimating the parameters of an HMM (POMDP) requires to sample a considerable amount of data, especially if the state space is very large. Algorithms for estimating parameters will certainly fail for continuous state spaces or continuous observation spaces. For these reasons, we think that it is not worth learning a model of a POMDP from data.

Despite these facts, there is some work available concerned with combining reinforcement learning with HMMs. Two of the early approaches coping with partial observability are presented in [Chr92] and [McC93]. Both algorithms learn a model by a variant of the Baum-Welch algorithm [BPSW70]. A simple approximation of the Q-function, equal to the dot product of the belief state with the vector of QMDP-values is used to extract a policy. The QMDP-values refer to the optimal Q-function on single states (MDP). The extracted policy is equivalent to the optimal policy on belief states only if the optimal Q-function on belief states can be represented by a single vector ($|\Gamma_0| = 1$). This is not the case except for the very simplest POMDPs. The two approaches differ in the way the state space is refined. In [Chr92], a state is split if the resulting model after a split is significantly different from the original model. In [McC93], a state is split if this will enable the learning agent to gain a higher cumulative reward.

4.2 Learning Suboptimal Policies based on Short-Term Memory

One important property shared by all approaches for solving POMDPs without a model is the difficulty of establishing theoretical guarantees with respect to the performance of the policies learned. In fact, it is very difficult to relate the learned policies to the optimal policy on belief states. In this section, we want to analyze how much memory is generally necessary for learning very good, but suboptimal policies. We will implement a model-free algorithm on history lists based on the idea of identifying a state by a sequence of past observations and actions. We choose history lists for this purpose, because the list concept is very simple and it is straightforward to quantify the memory allocated by a history list. Note that such an analysis would not be easy for other types of memory. For example, it is not clear how much memory is used by a recurrent neural network.

Since a history list is a finite sequence of past observations and actions, a history list can be regarded as an approximation of the current information state I_t. While the information state I_t contains the complete, possibly infinite sequence of past events, a history list contains only a small fraction of this sequence. In particular, we will define a history list to be a suffix of I_t.

4.2.1 A Partially Observable Maze

We will start with an illustrative example to explain the principal ideas of how history lists can be useful in a partially observable environment. The partially observable maze in Figure 4.4 will be used as a running example throughout the thesis. In later sections, we will also provide an empirical analysis for this maze.

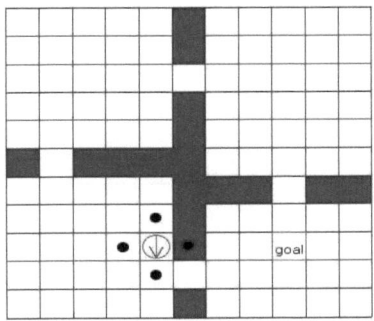

Figure 4.4: Maze with partial observability

In Figure 4.4, the learning agent is denoted by an arrow in a circle. The agent is expected to find a certain goal cell in the maze. To determine the current position of the agent, only four bump sensors are available. These sensors, denoted by black dots, can tell the agent if there are walls at the four surrounding cells. For instance, the first sensor detects a wall located above the agent, while the second sensor detects a wall located below the agent. An observation made by the agent corresponds to a combination of four distinct measurements provided by the four sensors. In Table 4.1, all possible observations are summarized.

The observation space therefore consists of sixteen combinations of walls plus an additional goal observation. Note that the observation model solely depends on the state of the process, expressed by a deterministic function $f_O : S \to O$. The action space contains four distinct actions for moving left, right, up or down (Table 4.2). If the agent tries to break through a wall or tries to leave the maze, the position of the agent remains the same.

How can the agent make use of history lists in this maze environment? The basic idea is to determine the current position of the agent by comparing history lists at different time steps. If the same sequence of past wall observations and actions is given at two time steps $t \neq t'$, it is likely that also the position of the agent is the same at these time steps ($s_t = s_{t'}$). We do not expect a history list

Observation	Sensor Values	Observation	Sensor Values
0	**goal**	9	below
1	no walls	10	left ∧ below
2	left	11	right ∧ below
3	right	12*	left ∧ right ∧ below
4	left ∧ right	13	below ∧ above
5	above	14*	left ∧ below ∧ above
6	left ∧ above	15*	right ∧ below ∧ above
7	right ∧ above	16*	walls everywhere
8*	left ∧ right ∧ above	-	-

Table 4.1: Possible observations in a POMDP maze. The first column gives the unique number of the observation and the second column gives the combination of walls detected by the sensors. The * symbol denotes a combination which is not present in the considered maze.

Action	Direction of Move
0	left
1	right
2	up
3	down

Table 4.2: Possible actions in a POMDP maze.

to contain the complete sequence of past observations and actions. In general, history lists can be of arbitrary length.

4.2.2 Basic Facts about History Lists

Our analysis of history lists will mainly concentrate on the deterministic case, since it is difficult to represent probabilities with history lists. The next chapter provides a discussion of how to scale our approach to the stochastic case. However, from now on, we assume that a deterministic partially observable Markov decision process $M := (T, S, A, O, f_S, f_O, r)$ is implicitly given. All objects referenced in the text, such as states, observations or actions, are part of this particular POMDP M.

Definition 16. *History List*
A history list $h \in (A \times O)^*$ is a finite, possibly empty sequence of action-observation pairs. The length $|h|$ of a history list is defined as the number of observations the sequence contains. The space of possible history lists $H^* \subseteq (A \times O)^*$ contains all history lists which can be generated by the transition model f_S and the observation model f_O. A history space $H \subset H^*$ is any finite subset of H^* including the empty sequence.

In Figure 4.5, the components of a history list are illustrated. The most recent observation made is located at the tail of the history list, while the oldest observation is located at the front. Note that for general observation models $f_O : A \times S \rightarrow O$, a history list begins with an action. However, if the observation model solely depends on the state ($f_O : S \rightarrow O$), we allow history lists to have an additional observation at the front, representing the observation of the initial state of the history sequence. Since many problems can be stated by such a simplified observation model, we will often use this type of observation model for examples and illustrations. We can show that all analysis presented for general history lists beginning with an action carries over to history lists beginning with an observation.

The concept of a history space $H \subset H^*$ is useful, because it enables us to restrict the length of the history lists considered. Since we want to implement short-term memory instead of perfect memory, it is undesirable to work on history lists of arbitrary length. In contrast to the information space, a history space is a finite set of reasonably short and carefully selected history lists. Moreover, a finite history space H allows storing statistics about every single element of H.

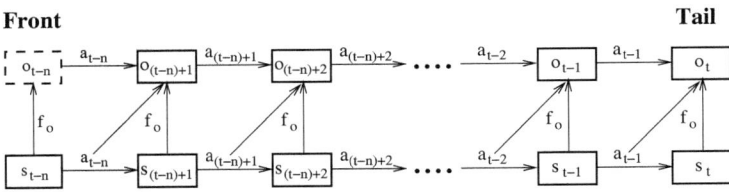

Figure 4.5: Components of a history list. A history list is a suffix of the complete sequence of past observations and actions (information state). The dashed observation o_{t-n} is included in the list only if the observation model f_O depends solely on the state ($f_O : S \rightarrow O$).

From a learning agent point of view, a history space $H \subset H^*$ serves as a replacement for the state space S, which is partially observable in a POMDP setting. The current state $s_t \in S$ is not visible to the agent, but only the information state I_t consisting of observations of actions. Since we introduced the history list concept as an approximation of the information state, it is reasonable to define the current history $h_t \in H$ as a fraction of the current information state I_t. Stated precisely, the current history h_t list is a suffix of I_t and an element of the history space H used.

55

Definition 17. *Suffix of a History List*
Let $h := [a_0, o_1, a_1, o_2, ..., a_{n-1}, o_n]$ be a history list of length n. A history list $h' := [a'_0, o'_1, a'_1, o'_2 ..., a'_{m-1}, o'_m]$ of length m is called a suffix of h, if $m \leq n$ and

$$\forall\, 0 \leq i \leq m-1 : a'_i = a_{i+(n-m)}$$

$$\forall\, 1 \leq i \leq m : o'_i = o_{i+(n-m)}$$

A suffix of a history list h is always a fraction of the tail of h. In particular, a history list is always a suffix of itself.

Definition 18. *Current History List*
Let $H \subset H^*$ be a history space and let $I_t := [a_0, o_1, a_1, o_2, ..., a_{t-1}, o_t]$ be the information state at time t generated by the transition model f_S and the observation model f_O. At time $t = 0$, the current history list h_0 is defined to be the empty sequence. At time $t > 0$, the current history list with respect to H and I_t is defined as
$h_t := \arg\max_{h \in H} \{|h|,\ h \text{ is a suffix of the composed sequence } [h_{t-1}, a_{t-1}, o_t]\}$.

The current history list $h_t \in H$ represents the maximal amount of information about past observations and actions contained in the history space H. Note, however, that h_t may be only a small fraction (suffix) of the complete information state I_t.

In order to develop a model-free algorithm based on history lists, two questions have to be answered.

1. Which history lists should be included into a history space H?

2. How it is possible to learn policies defined on a history space H?

We will first concentrate on the second question, assuming that a history space $H \subset H^*$ is already given. In subsequent sections, we will also present an algorithm for learning a history space H from sampled episodes.

We conjecture that a current history list $h_t \in H$ is especially useful if it helps to reduce uncertainty about the current state $s_t \in S$ of the process. Such a history list is called an identifying history list.

Definition 19. *Identifying History Lists*
A history list $h \in H^*$ is called identifying for a set of states $S' \subseteq S$, if $|h| > 0$, and the following condition holds for all finite sequences of states and actions $[s_0, a_0, s_1, a_1, ..., a_{t-1}, s_t]$ that can be generated by the transition model f_S: If h is a suffix of the sequence $[a_0, f_O(a_0, s_1), ..., a_{t-1}, f_O(a_{t-1}, s_t)]$, then it holds that $s_t \in S'$.

In the following, we will use the term "identifying history list" only in the context of single states ($|S'| = 1$), unless the set S' is explicitly specified.

A simple example for identifying history lists is illustrated in Figure 4.6. It is easy to verify that the considered POMDP is always in state s_2, if observation o_2 is made. Thus, the single observation o_2 constitutes an identifying history list for state s_2. By extending the list $[o_2]$ at the tail, it is also possible to build identifying history lists for the states s_1 and s_3. Note that there may be several identifying history lists for the same state. However, we selected a single identifying history list for each state.

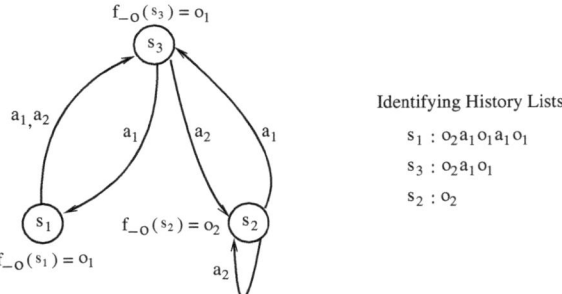

Figure 4.6: A deterministic POMDP with three states, two actions and two observations. The observations made solely depend on the state ($f_O : S \rightarrow O$). Next to the transition graph of the POMDP, a single identifying history list is built for each state.

Identifying history lists can also be found in the partially observable maze, as illustrated in Figure 4.7. The sequences of observations and actions corresponding to the three paths shown in Figure 4.7 uniquely identify the state of the agent. In contrast to the previous example, the history lists shown in Figure 4.7 identify the same state. Obviously, there are several identifying history lists

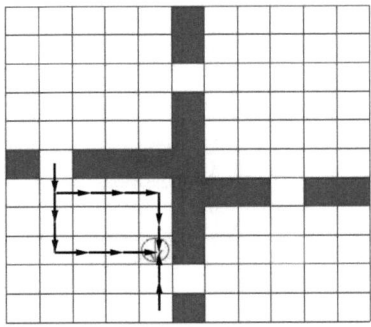

Figure 4.7: Three identifying history lists identifying the same cell in a partially observable maze. Each identifying history list is denoted by a sequence of black arrows.

for all maze cells.

Depending on the starting state of the process, there are a lot of different ways to identify the current state s_t. Since we want to maximize the information about the current state $s_t \in S$, it seems to be necessary to collect all identifying history lists and then label them with some state information. However, we will show in this thesis that it is possible to learn good policies with a much smaller set of history lists.

What makes identifying history lists especially interesting is the fact that these lists are closed under some typical list operations.

Lemma 4. *Extension of identifying history lists (at the front)*
Let $h \in H^*$ be an identifying history list for a set of states $S' \subseteq S$. If $h' \in H^*$ is an extension of h such that h is a suffix of h', then h' is identifying for the set of states S'.

Proof. Assume that h' is a suffix of a sequence $[a_0, o_1, ..., a_{t-1}, o_t]$ generated by the transition model f_S and the observation model f_O. Since h is a suffix of h', h is also a suffix of the sequence $[a_0, o_1, ..., a_{t-1}, o_t]$. Thus, it holds that $s_t \in S'$, because h is identifying for S'. □

Lemma 5. *Extension of identifying history lists (at the tail)*
Let $h \in H^*$ be an identifying history list for a single state $s \in S$. If $h' \in H^*$ is an extension of h such that an action $a \in A$ and an observation $o \in O$ is added at the tail of h, then h' is identifying for the single state $s' = f_S(s, a)$.

Proof. We assume that h' is a suffix of a sequence $[a_0, o_1, ...a_{t-2}, o_{t-1}, a_{t-1}, o_t]$ generated by the transition model f_S and the observation model f_O. By construction of h', it holds that $a = a_{t-1}$ and $o = o_t$. Moreover, history list h must be a suffix of the sequence $[a_0, o_1, ..., a_{t-2}, o_{t-1}]$. Since h is identifying for $s \in S$, it must hold that $s_{t-1} = s$. After action a_{t-1} has been executed, the next state is uniquely determined by the transition model f_S. Thus, it holds that $s_t = f_S(s_{t-1}, a_{t-1}) = f_S(s, a) = s'$. □

Comparison of History Lists with Belief States

Before presenting the details of our algorithm, we want to discuss the principal differences between history lists and belief states. Model-based algorithms for solving POMDPs are based on belief states, because belief states are equivalent to information states (Theorem 2). What is the loss of replacing perfect memory in the form of belief states by short-term memory in the form of history lists?

Similar to belief states, history lists are used to collect information about the current state s_t of the process. A belief state b_t gives, for every state $s \in S$ the probability $b_t(s)$ that s equals the current state. History lists are not capable of providing such detailed information. The current history list $h_t \in H$ enables us to draw one of the following three conclusions for every state $s \in S$.

1. State $s \in S$ equals the current state

2. State $s \in S$ possibly equals the current state

3. State $s \in S$ is different from the current state

If the current history h_t list identifies a single state $s \in S$, then we can conclude that s equals the current state s_t. Consequently, all other states $s' \neq s$ are different from the current state. Note that it is not known in advance if the current history lists h_t identifies a single state or not. This information must be inferred by a separate procedure. If the current history list h_t is identifying for a set of states S' with $|S'| > 1$, then for every state $s \in S'$ it holds that s possibly equals the current state s_t. All other states $s \in S \setminus S'$ are different from the current state.

History lists cause a drastic reduction of information compared to belief states. Exactly this reduction of information enables us to develop an efficient, model-free algorithm for solving POMDPs.

4.2.3 The Identify&Exploit Algorithm

A straightforward idea for applying history lists to POMDPs is to learn a policy $\pi : H \rightarrow A$, such that, whenever a history list $h \in H$ becomes the current history list at time t ($h = h_t$), then action $\pi(h)$ is executed. The Identify&Exploit algorithm presented in this section sticks to this idea, but with one important difference: The policy is restricted to identifying history lists. Since every identifying history list $h \in H$ corresponds to a state $s^h \in S$ identified by h, the optimal action for list h equals the optimal action for state s^h. These optimal actions can be inferred by learning a Q-function $\hat{Q} : H \times A \rightarrow \mathbb{R}$ defined on identifying history lists. A module of our algorithm, namely the exploitation module, consists of extracting greedy actions from the function $\hat{Q}$. The policy π learned by the Identify&Exploit algorithm is therefore a greedy policy derived from a Q-function.

To apply a policy learned, it seems to be necessary that all history lists from H identify a state. Fortunately, this is not the case. An identification module of our algorithm establishes exactly those states for which identifying history lists are available in H. The Identify&Exploit algorithm consists of two separate modules, constituting a two-phase procedure for solving deterministic POMDPs.

1. At time $t = 0$, a preferably short sequence of actions is executed such that the current history list $h_{t'}$ at time $t' \geq 0$ becomes identifying for the current state $s_{t'}$. This corresponds to establishing a belief state in which a single state $s \in S$ has probability $p(s) = 1$, while all other states have probability zero. This module is called the efficient identification strategy.

2. At time $t > t'$, follow a greedy policy extracted from a Q-function defined on identifying history lists. This is reasonable, since every identifying history list corresponds to a single state $s \in S$. If, at some time step later than t', the current history list becomes non-identifying, jump back to the first step of this enumeration (to reestablish an identifying history list). This module is called the exploitation module.

To implement a procedure as described above, it is necessary to have a criterion able to decide whether the current history list $h_t \in H$ is identifying the current state s_t or not. In other words, we need to have an exit condition for the identification module of the algorithm. Moreover, we need both a modified Q-learning procedure as well as an efficient identification strategy leading to an identifying history list. Here, to specify the complete algorithm, we assume that all these modules are already available. We also need the concept of a transition instance.

Definition 20. *Transition Instance*
Let $H \subset H^*$ be a history space and let $\mathcal{E} := [a_o, o_1, ..., a_{L-1}, o_L]$ be an episode of length L sampled from the transition model f_S and the observation model f_O. Let the corresponding sequence of system states of episode $\mathcal{E}$ be $[s_0, s_1, ..., s_L]$. The transition instance $\mathcal{T}_t$ on episode $\mathcal{E}$ at time $0 \leq t < L$ is given by the five-tuple $\mathcal{T}_t := (h_t, a_t, r_t, h_{t+1})$ with $r_t := r(s_t, a_t)$ and both $h_t \in H$ as well as $h_{t+1} \in H$ are current history lists with respect to the information states occuring on episode $\mathcal{E}$. A set of transition instances collected by sampling episodes will be denoted by the symbol $\mathcal{F}$. A set of transition instances $\mathcal{F}$ possibly contains transitions from several episodes.

We assume that a Q-function $\hat{Q} : H \times A \to \mathbb{R}$ has already been learned after sampling a set of transition instances $\mathcal{F}$. The details of the Q-learning procedure will be discussed shortly. We also assume that every history list $h \in H$ has been correctly classified as "identifying" or as "non-identifying". Since we want to learn Q-values only for identifying history lists, we introduce a set of valid actions $A_h^{vl} \subseteq A$ for every history list $h \in H$.

- The set of valid actions $A_h^{vl} \subseteq A$ for a history list $h \in H$ is defined to be empty, if h is non-identifying. Otherwise, the set A_h^{vl} contains action $a \in A$ if there exists a transition instance $(h_t = h, a_t = a, r_t, h_{t+1}) \in \mathcal{F}$ such that h_{t+1} is an identifying history list.

- The greedy action for $h \in H$ is computed with respect to the set of valid actions A_h^{vl}, i.e. by the expression $\arg\max_{a \in A_h^{vl}} \hat{Q}(h, a)$. If $A_h^{vl} = \emptyset$, the maximal Q-value $\max_{a \in A_h^{vl}} Q(h, a)$ is defined to be a large negative constant $-Q\_MAX\_CONST$. Thus, if no valid actions are available, history list $h \in H$ is marked as a dead end.

The definition of the set A_h^{vl} makes sure that a greedy action for $h \in H$ is available only if h identifies a state. Moreover, an action $a \in A$ is only included into A_h^{vl} if there exists an identifying successor list h_{t+1} of h. This additional condition ensures that the greedy policy never causes a transition to a non-identifying history list. The greedy policy should avoid running into dead ends, where transitions to other identifying history lists are impossible. However, if $A_h^{vl} = \emptyset$, it may be impossible to avoid such a transition to a non-identifying history list. The Identify&Exploit algorithm then chooses an action at random. In the undesirable event that a non-identifying history becomes the current history list, the Identify&Exploit algorithm switches back from the exploitation module to the identification module. The complete Identify&Exploit algorithm is illustrated by Algorithm 3.

Algorithm 3 Identify and Exploit
1: $\mathcal{E} \leftarrow [], h_0 \leftarrow []$
2: $a_0 \leftarrow Efficient\_Identification$
3: Execute action a_0
4: $t \leftarrow 1$
5: **loop**
6:     Observe $o_t \in O$
7:     Update representation of information state $I_t \leftarrow [a_0, o_1, ..., a_{t-1}, o_t]$
8:     Compute current history list $h_t \in H$ with respect to I_t
9:     **if** h_t is identifying and $A_{h_t}^{vl} \neq \emptyset$ **then**
10:         $a_t \leftarrow \arg\max_{a \in A_{h_t}^{vl}} \hat{Q}(h_t, a)$
11:     **else if** If h_t is identifying and $A_{h_t}^{vl} = \emptyset$ **then**
12:         $a_t \leftarrow$ random action (uniform distribution)
13:     **else if** h_t is non-identifying **then**
14:         $a_t \leftarrow Efficient\_Identification$
15:     **end if**
16:     Execute action a_t
17:     $t \leftarrow t + 1$
18: **end loop**

Safe Q-Learning on Identifying History Lists

The pseudocode for our modified Q-learning procedure is presented in Algorithm 4. Similar to ordinary Q-learning, exploration is randomized by an ϵ-greedy strategy. The constant $0 < \epsilon < 1$ is an additional parameter of the algorithm.

Since greedy actions are only available for identifying history lists, actions for non-identifying history lists are determined by the efficient identification strategy.

Updates of the Q-function are only made for transitions from the set of valid transitions $\mathcal{F}^{vl}$. The definition of $\mathcal{F}^{vl}$ ensures that the Q-function is only updated on sequences of identifying history lists. Thus, every update on a history list corresponds to an update on a single state from S. As discussed later in detail, this is a key idea for proving convergence of the Q-learning update loop.

The process of resampling transition instances and learning a Q-function is iterated in order to increase the performance of the exploration strategy. The main loop is terminated if the size of the set $\mathcal{F}$ exceeds a certain threshold. We named this procedure Safe Q-learning, because it is possible to prove that the Q-function converges to a unique fixed point. An initial version of this algorithm is described in [TR07b].

Algorithm 4 Safe Q-Learning on History Lists
1: $\mathcal{F} \leftarrow \emptyset$
2: $\forall h \in H, \forall a \in A : \hat{Q}(h, a) \leftarrow 0$
3: **repeat**
4:   Sample a set of transition instances $\mathcal{F}_{new}$ by a modified ϵ-greedy exploration strategy. The greedy action of a non-identifying history list is determined by the efficient identification strategy
5:   $\mathcal{F} \leftarrow \mathcal{F} \cup \mathcal{F}_{new}$
6:   $\forall h \in H$: Recompute the sets of valid actions A_h^{vl}
7:   $\mathcal{F}^{vl} \leftarrow \{(h_t, a_t, r_t, h_{t+1}) \in \mathcal{F} \mid a_t \in A_{h_t}^{vl}$ and h_{t+1} is identifying$\}$
8:   **repeat**
9:     **for all** $(h_t, a_t, r_t, h_{t+1}) \in \mathcal{F}^{vl}$ **do**
10:      $\hat{Q}(h_t, a_t) \leftarrow r_t + \beta \max_{a \in A_{h_{t+1}}^{vl}} \hat{Q}(h_{t+1}, a)$
11:    **end for**
12:   **until** $\hat{Q}$ converges
13: **until** the size of $\mathcal{F}$ exceeds a certain threshold

Efficient Identification Strategy

The purpose of the efficient identification strategy is to establish an identifying history list $h_t \in H$ by executing a sequence of actions. Here, efficient means that the identification strategy should find an identifying history with a high probability of success and with only a few number of steps. Thus, the procedure aims at minimizing the uncertainty about the current state. Note that the efficient identification strategy shown in Algorithm 5 again makes use of a criterion for detecting identifying history lists, although we have not presented such a criterion so far. We will address this issue in the next subsection.

The formulas needed to compute the identification strategy make use of the estimated transition matrices P_H^a defined on the history space H. If these matrices would represent Markov chains, the given procedure would perfectly approximate the probabilities of reaching an identifying history list. Unfortunately, the Markov property, $p(h_{t+1} \mid h_t, a_t) = p(h_{t+1} \mid h_t, a_t, h_{t-1}, ..., h_{t-n})$, does not hold for most history lists $h \in H$, especially if h does not identify a state. The procedure can be therefore regarded as a heuristic. However, our empirical results show that this particular heuristic is very successful for deterministic POMDPs.

Discussion

We want to discuss the performance of the Identify&Exploit algorithm compared to an optimal policy on belief states. It is easy to see that even if the identification strategy finds an identifying sequence of minimal length, the overall policy combining the efficient identification with the extracted greedy policy is still suboptimal. This is due to the fact that our approach does not take the reward signal into account while identifying the current state. The identifica-

Algorithm 5 Efficient Identification
1: Estimate a transition matrix P_H^a for every action $a \in A$ such that $p_{hh'}^a \in P_H^a$ gives the probability of a transition to history list $h' \in H$ after executing action $a \in A$ from history list $h \in H$. The probability $p_{hh'}^a$ is estimated by counting transition instances from $\mathcal{F}$ having the form $h \xrightarrow{a} h'$
2: Compute an action sequence probably leading to an identifying history list. This is implemented by considering action sequences of length L starting from the current history list $h_t \in H$. By inspecting the estimated transition model, every action sequence $[a_1, ..., a_L]$ reaching an identifying history list after at most L steps can be discovered and added to a candidate set. The parameter L is called the maximal search depth. Inspecting the transition model means performing a depth first search for identifying history lists in the transition graph of H derived from the transition matrices P_H^a. The search is started from the node representing the current history list h_t. Finally, the action sequence having the maximal probability of reaching an identifying history list is selected from the candidate set
3: The following equations can be used to compute the quantities needed. Here, $p(h_t, [a_1, ..., a_L])$ denotes the probability of reaching an identifying history list after at most L steps if action sequence $[a_1, ..., a_L]$ is executed from the current history list h_t. We computed these probabilities in an order corresponding to a depth first search in the transition graph of H.

$$p(h_t, []) = \begin{cases} 1, & \text{if } h_t \text{ is identifying} \\ 0, & \text{else} \end{cases}$$

$$p(h_t, [a_1, ..., a_L]) = \begin{cases} 1, & \text{if } h_t \text{ is identifying} \\ \sum_{h \in H} p_{h_t h}^{a_1} p(h, [a_2, ..., a_L]), & \text{else} \end{cases}$$

These equations can be used to compute the probabilities for all action sequences having a length of at most L, beginning with the empty sequence. Then, a final identification sequence is selected by the following expression

$$\arg\max_{[a_1,...,a_L]} p(h_t, [a_1, ..., a_L])$$

If several sequences have maximal probability, shorter sequences are preferred

tion module may cause very low rewards resulting in a loss of performance of the overall policy. The identification strategy actually implemented maximizes the probability of finding an identifying history list for the price of ignoring the cumulative reward. A straightforward extension of our identification procedure would be to estimate the reward function from transition instances and then perform value iteration on history lists. After a value function is learned, it is possible to derive a reward-optimal path to an identifying history list. However, this again would be a heuristic procedure, since value iteration relies on the Markov assumption $p(h_{t+1} \mid h_t, a_t) = p(h_{t+1} \mid h_t, a_t, h_{t-1}, ..., h_{t-n})$ as well.

There is another principal difference between the policy executed by the Identify&Exploit algorithm and an optimal policy on belief states. The Identify&Exploit algorithm strictly separates the two phases of identification and exploitation. The exploitation phase is given by a greedy policy extracted from a Q-function. An optimal policy, however, is able to mix up identification steps with greedy steps, thereby achieving two goals simultaneously. An optimal policy explores the partially observable environment in order to collect information about the current state, while solving the learning task at the same time. For example, consider the partially observable maze from Figure 4.4. A reasonable policy of the learning agent is to move to a corner in order to reduce uncertainty about the current state. However, an optimal policy is able to reduce uncertainty about the current state, while simultaneously approaching the goal state.

Detecting Identifying History Lists

We complete the specification of the Identify&Exploit algorithm by presenting a criterion for detecting identifying history lists. The criterion is well-suited for the purpose of analyzing how much memory is generally necessary for identifying the current state. A second criterion, which will be presented later, focuses on the practical aspects of learning policies in a partially observable environment.

Definition 21. *Criterion for Detecting Identifying History Lists (CC)*
Let $H \subset H^*$ be a history space. A history list $h \in H$ is called identifying according to criterion CC, if the following condition is satisfied:
$\nexists h' \in H : h' \neq h$ *and h is a suffix of h'.*

The criterion CC classifies a history list $h \in H$ as identifying if there is no other history list in H containing h as a suffix. How can this criterion be interpreted? Let $h := [a_0, o_1, ..., a_{L-1}, o_L]$ be a history list of length L. Assume that h becomes the current history list at time t, i.e. $h_t = h$. Thus, the sequence $h = [a_0, o_1, ..., a_{L-1}, o_L]$ is a suffix of the complete sequence of past observations and actions formed by the information state I_t. If there is no history list in H containing h as a suffix, then the history space H does not provide any information about events occurred before action a_0 was executed. Note that action a_0 does not mark the beginning of the information state I_t, but only the beginning of history list h. History list h is therefore maximally informative about the current state of the process with respect to history space H. In such a situation, h is supposed to identify this state.

In the following, we will provide an analysis on how to detect identifying history lists by criterion CC, given a finite state space. To cope with infinite state spaces, we will later introduce a second, alternative criterion for detecting identifying history lists.

How long must a history list be such that it is possible to identify an arbitrary state from S? The next definition establishes a lower bound.

Definition 22. *Sufficient History Length*
Let $M := (T, S, A, O, f_S, f_O, r)$ be a deterministic POMDP such that S is a finite set of states. The sufficient history length, l_{su}, is defined as

$$l_{su} := \begin{cases} \infty, & \text{if } \exists s \in S, \nexists h \in H^* : h \text{ identifies state } s \\ max_{s \in S} \min_{h \in H^*} \{|h|, h \text{ identifies state } s\}, & \text{else} \end{cases}$$

Given a sufficient history length $l_{su} < \infty$, it is possible to find an identifying history list no longer than l_{su} for an arbitrary state $s \in S$. If a history space $H \subset H^*$ does not contain sufficiently long history lists ($|h| \geq l_{su}$), it is impossible to identify every state from S. Note that the Identify&Exploit algorithm does not need to identify every single state. The identification module of the Identify&Exploit algorithm is designed to identify only those states for which identifying history lists are available. If criterion CC is used to guide the search for identifying history lists, the sufficient history length will turn out to be a critical parameter.

Lemma 6. *Bounds for the Sufficient History Length*
Let $M := (T, S, A, O, f_S, f_O, r)$ be a deterministic POMDP such that S is a finite set of states. If the transition graph of M induced by the transition function $f_S : S \times A \to S$ is strongly connected[2] and there is at least one state $s \in S$ for which an identifying history list $h \in H^*$ exists, then it holds that $l_{su} \leq |h| + |S|$.

Proof. Let h be an identifying history list for state $s \in S$. Consider an arbitrary state $s' \in S$. Since the transition graph of M is strongly connected, there exists a path from s to s'. Let h' be the action-observation sequence of this path. By extending h with h' (at the tail), we obtain an identifying history list for state s' (Lemma 5). Since any cycles on the path from s to s' can be removed, the path has a maximal length of $|S|$. Thus, the identifying history list for state s' has a maximal length of $|h| + |S|$. $\square$

The bounds of Lemma 6 are somewhat loose. However, the purpose of the lemma is to show that the sufficient history length is finite for a large class of deterministic POMDPs. For instance, the partially observable maze

---

[2] A transition graph is strongly connected if, for every pair $(s, s') \in S \times S$, it holds that there exists a path from s to s'.

from Figure 4.4 is a deterministic POMDP with a strongly connected transition graph. We think that the sufficient history length is finite for a much broader class of deterministic POMDPs, although we will not present further analysis with respect to this issue.

Before stating our main result with respect to criterion CC, we need to introduce a certain, especially favorable class of history spaces.

Definition 23. *Minimal Identifying History Lists*
An identifying history list $h \in H^*$ is called minimal, if there is no identifying history list $h' \neq h$, which is a suffix of h. Thus, it must hold that

$$\nexists h' \in H^* : h' \neq h \text{ and } h' \text{ is an identifying suffix of } h$$

Definition 24. *k-Complete History Spaces*
Let $H_k^{id} \subset H^*$ denote the set of identifying history lists for single states having a length less or equal to $k \in \mathbb{N}$. Let $H_k^{id^*} \subset H_k^{id}$ denote the subset of minimal identifying history lists contained in H_k^{id}. A history space $H \subset H^*$ is called k-complete if the following three conditions are satisfied:

$$H_{k-l_{su}}^{id^*} \subset H \tag{4.1}$$

$$\forall h \in H_k^{id^*} \setminus H_{k-l_{su}}^{id^*} \; \exists h' \in H : \; h' \text{ is a suffix of } h \text{ and } |h'| > k - l_{su} \tag{4.2}$$

$$\forall h \in H_{k-l_{su}}^{id^*} \; \nexists h' \in H : h' \neq h \text{ and } h \text{ is a suffix of } h' \tag{4.3}$$

A k-complete history space contains every minimal identifying history list up to a length of $k - l_{su}$ (condition 4.1). In addition, all extensions at the front of those minimal identifying history lists are explicity excluded (condition 4.3). For history lists longer than $k - l_{su}$, the requirements for a k-complete history space are lowered. A k-complete history space contains for every minimal identifying history list $h \in H_k^{id^*}$ longer than $k - l_{su}$ a suffix of this list (condition 4.2). Note that this suffix is not necessarily an identifying history list.

The definition of a k-complete history space reflects the necessity of having identifying history lists in the history space. Moreover, a k-complete history H space prefers minimal identifying history lists to very long history lists. The third condition in Definition 24 explicitly eliminates some identifying history lists from H which are not of minimal length.

Since the Identify&Exploit makes use of a criterion able to decide if a history list $h \in H$ is identifying or not, it is reasonable to ask how well criterion CC will do for this purpose. In other words, how does criterion CC affect the performance of the Identify&Exploit algorithm? Both the efficient identification strategy as well as the procedure for updating the Q-values (Algorithm 4) critically rely on a criterion for detecting identifying history lists.

Theorem 4. *Detection of Identifying History Lists with Criterion CC*
Let $H \subset H^*$ be a history space and let $h \in H$ be a history list of length $\hat{k} := |h|$. If $k - \hat{k} \geq l_{su}$ for a fixed $k \in \mathbb{N}$, then the following two propositions hold:

H is k-complete : h is identifying $\Rightarrow \nexists h' \in H : h' \neq h, h$ is a suffix of h'
(If H is k-complete, then criterion CC is complete)

H satisfies 4.1-2 : h is identifying $\Leftarrow \nexists h' \in H : h' \neq h, h$ is a suffix of h'
(If H satisfies the conditions (4.1) and (4.2), then criterion CC is correct)

Proof. ($\Rightarrow$):
Let $h \in H$ be an identifying history list and let $h^{id^*} \in H^*$ be the minimal identifying suffix of h. Since $|h^{id^*}| \leq |h| = \hat{k} \leq k - l_{su}$, it holds that $h^{id^*} \in H^{id^*}_{k-l_{su}}$. Since h^{id^*} is also a suffix of h, it follows from condition (4.3) that $h = h^{id^*}$. Thus, it holds that $h \in H^{id^*}_{k-l_{su}}$ and it follows again from condition (4.3) that there is no history list $h' \in H$ such that $h \neq h'$ and h is a suffix of h'.
($\Leftarrow$):
Let $[s_0, a_0, ..., s_{t-\hat{k}}, a_{t-\hat{k}}, ..., a_{t-1}, s_t]$ be a sequence of states and actions generated by the transition model f_S. Let $[a_0, o_1, ..., a_{t-\hat{k}}, o_{(t-\hat{k})+1}, ..., a_{t-1}, o_t]$ be the corresponding sequence of observations and actions generated by the observation model f_O. We assume that $h = [a_{t-\hat{k}}, o_{(t-\hat{k})+1}, ..., a_{t-1}, o_t]$ is a suffix of the sequence with $|h| = \hat{k}$. We assume further that h is a non-identifying history list. We have to show that there is at least one history list in H containing h as a suffix. By the definition of the sufficient history length l_{su}, there exists an identifying history list $h' \in H^*$, $h' := [a'_0, o'_1, ..., a'_{r-1}, o'_r]$ for state $s_{t-\hat{k}}$ with $r \leq l_{su}$. Consider the history list $h'' := [a'_0, o'_1, ..., a'_{r-1}, o'_r, a_{t-\hat{k}}, o_{(t-\hat{k})+1}, ..., a_{t-1}, o_t]$, which is built by extending h' with history list h (at the tail). The first thing to show is that $h'' \in H^*$, i.e. the history list h'' can be generated by the transition model f_S and the observation model f_O. Since h' is an identifying history list for state $s_{t-\hat{k}}$, it trivially holds that $h' \in H^*$. We assumed that the sequence $h = [a_{t-\hat{k}}, o_{(t-\hat{k})+1}, ..., a_{t-1}, o_t]$ can be generated from state $s_{t-\hat{k}}$ by the transition model f_s and the observation model f_O. Since h'' is a concatenation of history list h' and history list h, it must hold that $h'' \in H^*$. It follows from Lemma 5 that h'' is an identifying history list for state s_t, because h'' is an extension of the identifying history list h'. Let h^{id^*} be the minimal identifying suffix of h''. Since both h^{id^*} and h are a suffix of h'', it must hold that either h is a suffix of h^{id^*} or h^{id^*} is a suffix of h. If h^{id^*} is a suffix of h (including the case $h = h^{id^*}$), then it follows from Lemma 4 that h is an identifying history list. This would be a contradiction to our assumption that h is a non-identifying history list. Thus, it must hold that h is a suffix of h^{id^*} with $h \neq h^{id^*}$. If $|h^{id^*}| \leq k - l_{su}$, then it holds that $h^{id^*} \in H^{id^*}_{k-l_{su}}$ and it follows from condition (4.1) that $h^{id^*} \in H$. In this case, we are finished, since h is a suffix of h^{id^*}. If $|h^{id^*}| > k - l_{su}$, then h^{id^*} has a length of at most k, because $|h| = \hat{k}, |h'| \leq l_{su}$, $|h''| = |h| + |h'|$ and $k \geq \hat{k} + l_{su}$. Thus, it holds that $h^{id^*} \in H^{id^*}_k \setminus H^{id^*}_{k-l_{su}}$.

It follows from condition (4.2) that there exists a suffix $h''' \in H$ of h^{id^*} with $|h'''| > k - l_{su}$. Since h is a suffix of h^{id^*} and $|h| < |h'''|$, h must be a suffix of h''' with $h \neq h'''$. Thus, we found a history list in H containing h as a suffix. □

Note that for a k-complete history space H, both directions of Theorem 4 hold, since the conditions (4.1) and (4.2) immediately follow from the definition of a k-complete history space. Note also that for applying criterion CC, it is not necessary to know the exact value of l_{su}. An overestimation of l_{su} will not affect the proof of the theorem.

If a k-complete history space H is available, then criterion CC will work perfectly for history lists $h \in H$ no longer than $k - l_{su}$. For this to show, let $H_{k-l_{su}} \subset H^*$ denote the set of history lists no longer than $k - l_{su}$. The subset $H^{id}_{k-l_{su}} \subseteq H_{k-l_{su}}$ contains all identifying history lists from $H_{k-l_{su}}$. The second proposition of Theorem 4 guarantees that criterion CC will never classify a history list $h \in H_{k-l_{su}}$ as identifying if this is not truly the case. We consider this to be a correctness result. The first proposition of Theorem 4 guarantees that all identifying history lists $h \in H^{id}_{k-l_{su}}$ are actually detected by criterion CC. We consider this to be a completeness result. Thus, if the history space H used by the Identify&Exploit algorithm is k-complete, we expect both the Safe Q-Learning procedure (Algorithm 4) as well as the efficient identification strategy to work properly. If a history list $h \in H$ is longer than $k - l_{su}$, then h is assumed to be non-identifying, since Theorem 4 cannot be applied to h.

Interestingly, criterion CC is still "correct" even if H is not k-complete. The proof of the second proposition of Theorem 4 relies on the somewhat weaker assumption that the conditions (4.1) and (4.2) are satisfied. What does this mean for the Safe Q-Learning algorithm and the efficient identification strategy?

The idea of the Safe Q-Learning algorithm is to perform Q-learning updates only for identifying history lists. Thus, the updates of the Safe Q-Learning algorithm are correct as long as criterion CC is correct (second proposition of Theorem 4). However, even if criterion CC works correctly, the learned Q-function is not guaranteed to be useful. There may be many identifying history lists excluded from updating the Q-function. For example, consider a trivial history space $H := H_k$ containing all history lists up to length k. Thus, both conditions (4.1) and (4.2) are trivially satisfied and criterion CC is guaranteed to work correctly. However, it is still possible that criterion CC classifies a history list as non-identifying, although the list actually identifies a state. In fact, criterion CC will classify all history lists from $H = H_k$ as non-identifying and no Q-learning updates will be processed at all. In order to achieve a good performance of criterion CC, a history space H should contain many minimal identifying history lists, but no extensions of these lists. If the history space H contains no front extensions of identifying history lists at all, H is k-complete by Definition 24. The performance of the Safe Q-Learning procedure gradually improves with the quality of the history spaces used. Perfect performance is achieved for a k-complete history space as reflected by Theorem 4. Learning such history spaces is therefore an important issue, which will be discussed later.

Similar arguments apply to the efficient identification strategy. The identification strategy is basically an uninformed search in a directed graph. The nodes in this graph correspond to history lists and the goal of the search is to find a node corresponding to an identifying history list. If criterion CC works correctly, but H is not k-complete, some identifying history lists will not be recognized as valid goals in the graph. This is due to the fact that criterion CC will mistakenly classify some identifying history lists as non-identifying. However, the length of a shortest path to a goal node strongly depends on the total number of goal nodes present in the graph. Thus, the length of the action sequence computed by the identification strategy depends on the quality of the history space H. If H contains many front extensions of minimal identifying history lists, only a few goal nodes are present in the graph. Conversely, if the history space used is k-complete, every identifying history list will be recognized as a valid goal.

To summarize, the key for successfully detecting identifying history lists is to concentrate on identifying history lists of minimal length. If the history space H used consists solely of minimal identifying suffixes, criterion CC is able to do a perfect classification. However, if front extensions of minimal identifying history lists are present in H, the performance of criterion CC is limited.

If the observation model solely depends on the current state ($f_O : S \to O$), then Theorem 4 also holds for history lists $h = [o_0, u_0, .., u_{t-1}, o_t]$, including the observation of the initial state of the history sequence. A modified proof of Theorem 4 can be found in the appendix.

Safe Q-Learning on Complete History Spaces

Further analysis of the Identify&Exploit algorithm will concentrate on two aspects.

1. Under which circumstances will the Safe Q-Learning algorithm converge to a unique greedy policy?

2. Is it possible to analyze the performance of the greedy policy learned?

The following theorem gives answers to both of the questions above. The proof is quite lengthy, because we want it to include illustrative arguments enabling a better understanding of some of the key ideas of the Identify&Exploit algorithm.

Theorem 5. *Convergence of Q-Learning on k-Complete History Spaces*
Let $M := (T, S, A, O, f_S, f_O, r)$ be a deterministic partially observable Markov decision process such that S is a finite set of states. Let $0 \le \beta < 1$ be a discounting rate and let $k \in \mathbb{N}$ be a fixed constant. If $H \subset H^*$ is a history space for which it holds that H satisfies the conditions (4.1) and (4.2), and criterion CC is used to detect identifying history lists from H, then the Safe Q-Learning algorithm (Algorithm 4) will converge to a unique Q-function. Moreover, there exists a deterministic MDP M_H such that the greedy policy extracted from the Q-Function constitutes an optimal policy for M_H.

Proof. The proof consists of two parts. In the first part, we will construct a deterministic MDP M_H such that all Q-learning updates performed by Algorithm 4 are equivalent to ordinary Q-learning updates on the MDP M_H. The second part shows that these Q-learning updates converge to a fixed point such that an optimal policy for M_H can be extracted from the learned Q-function $\hat{Q}$.

The first thing to show is that the set of sampled transition instances $\mathcal{F}$ converges to a final set $\mathcal{F}_\infty$, consisting of all possible transitions (h_t, a_t, r_t, h_{t+1}) which can be generated by the transition model f_S and the observation model f_O. This is due to the fact that at every time $t \in T$, the sampling strategy selects every action $a \in A$ with at least probability $\epsilon > 0$. Thus, every possible transition on history lists, given the finite state space S, the finite action space A, and the finite history space H, will eventually occur on a sampled episode. Note that this final set of transition instances $\mathcal{F}_\infty$ is again finite.

We will now discuss the individual components of the constructed MDP $M_H := (T_H, S_H, A_H, f_H, r_H)$, based on the final set of transition instances $\mathcal{F}_\infty$. In the following, the set $\mathcal{F}^{vl}$ denotes the set of valid transitions derived from the set $\mathcal{F}_\infty$. See Algorithm 4 for the definition of the set $\mathcal{F}^{vl}$.

Time Steps The set of time steps is adopted from the POMDP M ($T_H := T$).

State Space The state space of M_H consists of a set of history lists $S_H \subseteq H$. Stated more precisely, S_H contains all history lists $h \in H, |h| \le k - l_{su}$ classified as identifying according to criterion CC. We assume that all other history list are classified as non-identifying.

It follows from Theorem 4 that every history list in S_H is an identifying history list for a single state from S.

Actions The actions are adopted from the POMDP M ($A_H := A$). However, the set of actions executable from a history list $h \in S_H$ is restricted to the set $A_h^{vl} \subseteq A$. In subsection 4.2.3, a procedure is given to compute the set A_h^{vl} from the final set of sampled transition instances $\mathcal{F}_\infty$.

Transition Model The transition model $f_H : S_H \times A_H \to S_H$ is deterministic. We define $f_H(h, a) := h'$ for history list $h \in S_H$ and an action $a \in A_h^{vl}$ if there exists a transition instance $(h_t = h, a_t = a, r_t, h_{t+1} = h') \in \mathcal{F}^{vl}$. From the definition of the set A_h^{vl}, it follows that there exists at least one such transition instance $(h_t = h, a_t = a, r_t, h_{t+1} = h') \in \mathcal{F}^{vl}$ with $h \in S_H$.

It remains to show that f_H is well-defined and $h' \in S_H$. We assume a sampled transition instance $(h_t = h, a_t = a, r_t, h_{t+1} = h') \in \mathcal{F}^{vl}$ generated by the transition model f_S and the observation model f_O. We have to show that whenever $h \in H$ becomes the current history list $(h_t = h)$, and action $a \in A_h^{vl}$ is executed $(a_t = a)$, the successor list is uniquely given by $h_{t+1} = h' \in H$. Since every history list in S_H is identifying a state, we can conclude that history list h identifies a state $s^h \in S$. Thus, it holds that $s_t = s^h$ if $h_t = h$. If action $a \in A_h^{vl}$ is executed from h, then it holds that $s' := s_{t+1} = f_S(s^h, a)$ and $o' := o_{t+1} = f_O(a, s')$. It follows that whenever $h \in H$ becomes the current history list and action $a \in A_h^{vl}$ is executed, the successor list $h_{t+1} = h'$ will be computed based on a unique action-observation sequence. This sequence is given by $[h, a, o']$. The current history list h_{t+1} at time $t+1$ is defined as the maximal suffix of $[h, a, o']$ contained in H. Thus, the successor list $h_{t+1} = h'$ is uniquely determined.

It also holds that $h' \in S_H$. Since $(h_t = h, a_t, r_t, h_{t+1} = h') \in \mathcal{F}^{vl}$ and we showed that $h' \in H$ is the unique successor list of $h \in H$ after executing $a \in A_h^{vl}$, it must hold that $h' \in S_H$ by the definition of the set A_h^{vl}.

Reward Function Consider a history list $h \in S_H$ and an action $a \in A_h^{vl}$. Since the state space S_H contains solely identifying history lists, the history list h must identify a state $s^h \in S$. The reward function $r_H : S_H \times A_H \to \mathbb{R}$ is defined as $r_H(h, a) := r(s^h, a)$.

Since both functions f_H and r_H are deterministic, the process M_H is a deterministic Markov decision process (MDP). We will show that the Q-learning updates performed by Algorithm 4 are equivalent to ordinary Q-learning updates on M_H. An ordinary Q-learning update is defined in Algorithm 1 ($\alpha = 1$).
($\Rightarrow$): Assume that an update is made by Algorithm 4 for a transition instance $(h_t = h, a_t = a, r_t, h_{t+1} = h') \in \mathcal{F}^{vl}$. It immediately follows from the definition of Algorithm 4 that $a \in A_h^{vl}$ and $h' \in S_H$. From the definition of the set A_h^{vl}, it also follows that $h \in S_H$. Since h is identifying a state s^h, it holds that $r_t = (s^h, a) = r_H(h, a)$. Thus, the Q-learning update performed by Algorithm 4 is an ordinary Q-learning update on MDP M_H.
($\Leftarrow$): Assume a history list $h \in S_H$ and an action $a \in A_h^{vl}$ such that $h' := f_H(h, a)$ and $r' := r_H(h, a)$. These are the components of an ordinary Q-learning update for MDP M_H. It follows from the definition of the transition model f_H that there exists a transition instance $\mathcal{T} := (h_t = h, a_t = a, r_t, h_{t+1} = h') \in \mathcal{F}^{vl}$. Thus, an ordinary Q-learning update on MDP M_H is performed by Algorithm 4 for transition $\mathcal{T}$. Since $h \in S_H$ is identifying a state s^h, the reward signal r_t of the update made is equal to the reward signal $r_H(h, a)$ of the MDP M_H.

The second part of the proof is derived from the convergence proof for Q-learning given in [Mit97]. Note that this proof already covers the constructed MDP M_H. However, for the sake of completeness, we will present an adaptation of this proof using the notation of this thesis. In [BT96], an analysis is provided for the undiscounted case ($\beta = 1$).

We know from subsection 2.3.1 that in the case of discounted MDPs, an optimal policy π^* for the infinite horizon is stationary and deterministic. In particular, this also holds for M_H, since M_H is a deterministic MDP. Let π_H^* be an optimal policy with respect to M_H and let Q_H^* be the optimal Q-function. The following Bellman equation is a special (deterministic) case of Equation (2.9).

$$\forall h \in S_H, a \in A_h^{vl} : Q_H^*(h,a) = r_H(h,a) + \beta \max_{a' \in A_{f_H(h,a)}^{vl}} Q_H^*(f_H(h,a), a') \quad (4.4)$$

Let $\Delta_N := \max_{h \in S_H, a \in A_h^{vl}} |\hat{Q}^N(h,a) - Q_H^*(h,a)|$. Here, the function $\hat{Q}^N$ denotes the approximation of the optimal Q-function Q_H^* after the N-th iteration of updating all list-action pairs $(h,a) \in (S_H, A_h^{vl})$ in the update loop of Algorithm 4. The basic idea of the proof is to show that $\lim_{N \to \infty} \Delta_N = 0$. For all iterations $N \in \mathbb{N}$, for all history lists $h \in S_H$ and for all actions $a \in A_h^{vl}$, the following equations hold:

$$\begin{aligned}
|\hat{Q}^{N+1}(h,a) - Q_H^*(h,a)| &= |(r_H(h,a) + \beta \max_{a' \in A_{f_H(h,a)}^{vl}} \hat{Q}^N(f_H(h,a), a')) - \\
& \quad (r_H(h,a) + \beta \max_{a' \in A_{f_H(h,a)}^{vl}} Q_H^*(f_H(h,a), a'))| \\
&= \beta | \max_{a' \in A_{f_H(h,a)}^{vl}} \hat{Q}^N(f_H(h,a), a')) \\
& \quad - \max_{a' \in A_{f_H(h,a)}^{vl}} Q_H^*(f_H(h,a), a'))| \\
&\leq \beta \max_{a' \in A_{f_H(h,a)}^{vl}} |\hat{Q}^N(f_H(h,a), a')) \\
& \quad - Q_H^*(f_H(h,a), a'))| \\
&\leq \beta \max_{h' \in S_H, a' \in A_{h'}^{vl}} |\hat{Q}^N(h',a') - Q_H^*(h',a')| \\
&= \beta \Delta_N \quad (4.5)
\end{aligned}$$

The first equality is derived from the Bellman equation (4.4) and the definition of the Safe Q-learning algorithm (Algorithm 4).

From the last equality, it follows that the maximal difference Δ_N between the approximated Q-function after N iterations and the optimal Q-function is at most $\beta^N \Delta_0$. This can be easily shown by an inductive argument. The largest initial error Δ_0 is bounded because both $\hat{Q}_0$ and Q_H^* are bounded. The approximated Q-function $\hat{Q}_0$ is bounded because the initial Q-function is initialized with constant values. The optimal Q-function Q_H^* is bounded because $Q_H^*(h,a) = r_H(h,a) + \sum_{t=1}^{\infty} \beta^t r(h_t, \pi_H^*(h_t))$ with $h_t = f_H(h_{t-1}, a)$ and $h_1 = f_H(h,a)$. Since the reward function is also bounded, there exists a constant C with $Q_H^*(h) \leq C \sum_{t=1}^{\infty} \beta^t = C \frac{1}{1-\beta}$. Thus, it holds that $\lim_{N \to \infty} \beta^N \Delta_0 = 0$ and therefore $\lim_{N \to \infty} |\hat{Q}^N(h,a) - Q_H^*(h,a)| = 0$. □

4.2.4 Learning Complete History Spaces

Before a policy defined on history lists can be learned, it is necessary to select a set of history lists constituting a history space H. As already pointed out, a k-complete history space enables the Identify&Exploit algorithm to perfectly decide if a history list is identifying or not. Moreover, a k-complete history space forces the Safe Q-Learning algorithm to converge to a unique fixed point. We will now present a procedure able to learn such history spaces.

The basic idea of this procedure has already been introduced in [HJ06] for the purpose of learning a prediction suffix tree. We will show that the idea also applies to learning k-complete history spaces. In contrast to [HJ06], we also consider the reward signals. To understand how the algorithm works, it is instructive to make the following observation. In a deterministic POMDP, the sequence of observations and rewards is uniquely determined, given a starting state and a sequence of actions. Thus, whenever an identifying history list becomes the current history list, the following sequence of observations and rewards is unique, given a fixed action sequence. This simple insight can be used to incrementally build a k-complete history.

First, a set of episodes is sampled from the underlying POMDP. If a history list $h \in H$ becomes the current history list ($h = h_t$), it can be checked f or a fixed action sequence starting at time t if the corresponding sequence of observations and rewards is uniquely determined with respect to the sampled episodes. If this is the case for all action sequences occurring on these episodes, h is considered to be identifying and will not be extended any further. Otherwise, the history list h is extended by an additional action-observation pair. Remember that a k-complete history space does not include front extensions of identifying history lists. Thus, we only extend a history list if the list is supposed to be non-identifying. Algorithm 6 shows pseudocode of this procedure.

Lemma 7. *Learning Minimal Identifying History Lists*
Let $H \subset H^*$ be a history space learned by Algorithm 6. Let $H^{id^*}_{k-l_{su}}$ denote the set of minimal identifying history lists up to length of $k - l_{su}$. If $h \in H \cap H^{id^*}_{k-l_{su}}$, then H does not include any front extensions of history list h.

Proof. Consider the case in which an identifying history list h' has been added to the candidate set H_c such that h' is a front extension of a minimal identifying history list $h \in H \cap H^{id^*}_{k-l_{su}}$. Since h is identifying a state s^h, the set of sampled episodes $\mathcal{F}$ is deterministic for h. This can be shown by the following argument: Consider two episodes $\mathcal{E} \in \mathcal{F}, \mathcal{E}' \in \mathcal{F}$ in which h becomes the current history list at time t and t', respectively. Thus, it must hold that $s_t = s_{t'} = s^h$. Since we assumed a deterministic transition model f_S and a deterministic observation model f_O, the sequences of observations and rewards starting from t and t' are the same if the corresponding action sequences are the same. Thus, $\mathcal{F}$ is deterministic for h and Algorithm 6 will not add h' to H. □

A history list $h \in H$ is extended by Algorithm 6 until the set $\mathcal{F}$ becomes deterministic for h. If the set $\mathcal{F}$ becomes deterministic for a history list $h \in H$, the list is supposed to be identifying for a state.

Algorithm 6 Learning k-Complete History Spaces

1: A set $\mathcal{F}$ containing sampled episodes is called deterministic for a history list $h \in H$ if the following condition is satisfied: If h becomes the current history list on two different episodes from $\mathcal{F}$, then it holds that the following sequences of observations and rewards on the two episodes are the same if the corresponding action sequences are the same. Here, the following sequence means the sequence starting exactly at the time the history list h becomes the current history list
2:   $l \leftarrow 0$
3:   $H \leftarrow \{[ao] \mid a \in A, o \in O\}$
4: **repeat**
5:     $l \leftarrow l + 1$
6:     $\mathcal{F} \leftarrow \emptyset,\ H_c \leftarrow \emptyset$
7:     Collect new data by sampling a number of episodes completely at random. All sampled transition instances are stored in the set $\mathcal{F}$
8:     Build all one-step extensions (at the front and at the tail) of all history lists in H having a size of exactly l. One step means a single action-observation pair. Only those extensions are considered which actually occur on sampled episodes. The extended lists are added the to a candidate set H_c
9:     If a candidate list $h \in H_c$ is not a front extension of any history list $h' \in H, |h'| \leq k - l_{su}$ such that $\mathcal{F}$ is deterministic for h', then add h to H. Otherwise, discard h
10: **until** l=k

In order to prevent some identifying history lists from being overlooked by the sampling process, we consider extensions both at the front as well as at the tail of a history list. Lemma 7 shows that for all minimal identifying suffixes $h \in H_{k-l_{su}}^{id*}$ included into H, no front extensions are added to H. As can be seen from Definition 24, this is a critical aspect of learning a k-complete history space. Note that the condition stated in line 9 of the algorithm exactly matches condition (4.3) of Definition 24.

The only way Algorithm 6 can fail to learn a k-complete history space is if some minimal identifying history are left out. In such a case, the missing sequences of observations and actions did not occur in the sampled episodes. A reasonable solution to this problem is to increase the number of sampled episodes. However, if a sequence of actions and observations almost never occurs in sampled episodes, leaving out this sequence will presumably not damage the performance of the Identify&Exploit algorithm.

4.2.5 Empirical Analysis of Partially Observable Mazes

As a benchmark problem for testing the Identify&Exploit algorithm, we used the partially observable maze shown in Figure 4.4. The number of non-obstacle cells in the maze is 104, resulting in a state space of size $|S| = 104$. This is rather large compared to typical POMDP benchmarks from the literature. Moreover, it holds that $|O| = 12$ and $|A| = 4$. The reward function is defined to be -1 at all non-goal states and zero at the goal state. The goal state is absorbing such that no action will leave the goal state once the learning agent has found this state. Thus, the learning task is equivalent to finding the goal in minimal time.

The observations made by the learning agent do not depend on actions, but only on the current state. We therefore used history lists with an additional observation at the front. Since there are many cells in the maze having no walls surrounding them, it is necessary to take a couple of well-advised steps to identify the current state. In fact, we will show that it holds $l_{su} = 5$ for this particular POMDP.

Optimal Policies

For comparison, we first tackled the maze by model-based algorithms for solving POMDPs optimally. Unfortunately, we were not able to compute an optimal policy. Since the state space contains more than one hundred states, the computational effort for finding the optimal value function becomes intractable. We therefore conducted additional experiments for a smaller maze consisting of the lower right part of the original maze. The small maze has only a single room containing twenty cells ($|S| = 20$).

To compute an optimal value function for the small maze, we used the Witness algorithm from [LCK95]. The initial belief state for testing the policy extracted from the optimal value function was built according to a special distribution of initial states. We assume that the initial states are uniformly distributed, i.e. every non-obstacle cell of the maze has the same probability of being selected as an initial state. Such a choice of an initial belief state is reasonable, since we tested the policy from every non-obstacle cell exactly once.

To illustrate the complexity of both mazes, we also computed optimal policies for the fully observable case (MDP) allowing the learning agent to observe its exact position in the maze. For this purpose, we applied the Q-learning algorithm stated in Algorithm 1. In Table 4.3, we summarized the results. It

Maze	State Space ($|S|$)	MDP (optimal)	Witness (optimal)
Small	20	2.2	2.7
Big	104	7.77	?

Table 4.3: Performance of optimal policies. The third column corresponds to an optimal policy for the fully observable case (MDP), while the fourth column corresponds to an optimal policy for the partially observable case (POMDP). Both columns give the number of steps to the goal averaged over every possible starting state. A state s a possible starting state if it is a non-obstacle cell.

is easy to see that the performance of an optimal policy for the fully observable case bounds the performance of an optimal policy for the partially observable case. Although we are not able to provide exact values with respect to the big maze, we speculate that an optimal policy takes approximately nine to eleven steps to the goal.

Memoryless Policies

To point out the necessity of using memory to solve the partially observable mazes, we also computed the best memoryless policies. To interpret the results we achieved, it is instructive to refer to the concept of a proper policy introduced in [BT96]. We call a policy π proper if π is capable of reaching the goal state from every starting state. Since both mazes are deterministic, this definition of a proper policy is equivalent to the one given in [BT96].

Table 4.4 shows results from applying a model-based search (Branch & Bound) for optimal, memoryless policies. A detailed description of this algorithm is given in [Lit94]. The algorithm is guaranteed to eventually find an optimal solution and terminates after inspecting at most $|A|^{|O|}$ distinct policies.

For the small maze, it was possible to compute policies being both proper and memoryless. However, these policies have poor performance compared to the optimal policies from Table 4.3. We discovered that there exists no policy for the big maze, which is both proper and memoryless.

Learning Memoryless Policies without a Model

An algorithm similar to Q-learning, which has been already proven to be successful in model-free learning memoryless policies for POMDPs, is the Sarsa(λ) algorithm ($0 \leq \lambda \leq 1$). The success of Sarsa(λ) is due to the fact that Sarsa(λ) is a mixture of Q-learning and a Monte Carlo approach for evaluating policies.

Maze	State Space ($|S|$)	Goal	Memoryless (optimal)
Small	20	100 %	7.9
Big	104	50.96 %	103.08

Table 4.4: Performance of optimal, memoryless policies. The third column gives the percentage of starting states from which the optimal policy reaches the goal state. The fourth column gives the number of steps to the goal averaged over every possible starting state. An episode for testing the learned policy is aborted if the goal state is not reached after at most 200 steps.

It is shown in [LS98] that, for $\lambda \approx 1$, Sarsa(λ) can handle POMDPs much better

---
Algorithm 7 Sarsa(λ)

1: $\forall o \in O, \forall a \in A : \hat{Q}(o,a) \leftarrow 0$
2: $\forall o \in O, \forall a \in A : e(o,a) \leftarrow 0$
3: $t \leftarrow 0$
4: Select initial learning rate $0 < \alpha_0 \leq 1$
5: Make initial observation o_0 of state s_0
6: Select random action a_0 and observe reward r_0
7: $t \leftarrow 1$
8: **repeat**
9:    Make observation o_t of state s_t
10:   Select action a_t by an ϵ-greedy exploration strategy
11:   $\delta \leftarrow r_{t-1} + \beta \hat{Q}(o_t, a_t) - \hat{Q}(o_{t-1}, a_{t-1})$
12:   $e(o_{t-1}, a_{t-1}) \leftarrow e(o_{t-1}, a_{t-1}) + 1$
13:   **for all** $o \in O, a \in A$ **do**
14:     $\hat{Q}(o,a) \leftarrow \hat{Q}(o,a) + \alpha_{t-1} \delta e(o,a)$
15:     $e(o,a) \leftarrow \beta \lambda e(o,a)$
16:   **end for**
17:   Update learning rate $\alpha_t \leftarrow h(\alpha_{t-1})$
18:   Observe reward $r_t \leftarrow r(s_t, a_t)$
19:   $t \leftarrow t + 1$
20: **until** the Q-function converges or t exceeds a certain threshold

---

than Q-learning.

The basic idea for learning memoryless policies by Sarsa(λ) is to approximate a Q-function on observations instead of states. Unfortunately, as for most POMDPs, the observation spaces of the mazes considered are not Markovian. While Q-learning is supposed to diverge in such a setting, the Sarsa(λ) algorithm may find good policies. A more detailed explanation of Sarsa(λ) is provided in [SB98].

We applied Sarsa(λ) to both mazes in order to figure out what memoryless policies can be learned without a model. Figure 4.8 shows a learning curve for Sarsa(λ) applied to the small maze. As for all learning curves presented in this thesis, the speed of the learning process is expressed in terms of control cycles. A control cycle corresponds to a single transition instance sampled. The total number of control cycles is therefore equivalent to the total number of interactions with the environment.

As for all of the following experiments, the optimal setting of parameters was found by a systematic search we had done before starting the final experiment. As proposed in [LS98], we implemented a linearly decreasing exploration rate. In particular, the exploration rate starts at $\epsilon = 0.4$ and then decreases linearly until the 10000th action is executed. After 10000 action choices, the exploration rate arrives at $\epsilon = 0$. The experiment consists of twenty runs. The learning curve shows the average performance of these runs supplemented by the standard deviation.

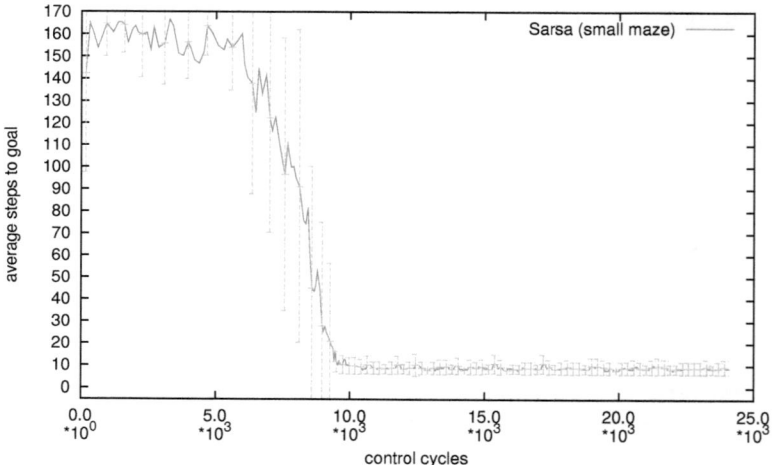

Figure 4.8: Learning memoryless policies for the small maze by Sarsa(λ). The x-axis shows the number of control cycles, while the y-axis shows the average number of steps to the goal. The number of steps to the goal is averaged over all possible starting states. Setting of parameters: Learning rate $\alpha = 0.01$, exploration rate $\epsilon = 0.4$ (linearly decreasing), discounting rate $\beta = 1$, and $\lambda = 0.9$.

Figure 4.9 shows a similar experiment for the big maze. Since the big maze contains many more cells, the exploration decreases much slower, i.e. the exploration rate arrives at $\epsilon = 0$ after 100000 action choices. Again, the setting of parameters was found by a systematic search and the experiment was repeated twenty times.

To summarize the results achieved, Table 4.5 shows for both experiments the final, average performance of the policies learned. Note that for the big

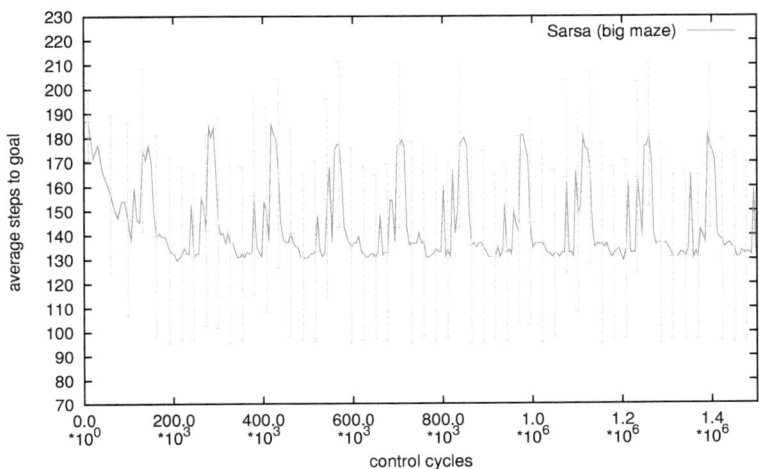

Figure 4.9: Learning memoryless policies for the big maze by Sarsa(λ). The x-axis shows the number of control cycles, while the y-axis shows the average number of steps to the goal. The number of steps to the goal is averaged over all possible starting states. Setting of parameters: Learning rate $\alpha = 0.01$, exploration rate $\epsilon = 0.4$ (linearly decreasing), discounting rate $\beta = 1$, and $\lambda = 0.95$.

maze, Sarsa(λ) turns out to be very unstable. This is probably due to the fact that there exists no memoryless policy capable of reaching the goal from every starting state.

The QU-List Algorithm

To compare our approach to another powerful method for solving POMDPs without a model, we conducted experiments with an extension of the U-tree algorithm [McC95]. In order to make the U-tree algorithm applicable to large state spaces, we added some features to U-tree. We named this extended algorithm QU-List. Both U-tree and QU-list compare well to the Identify&Exploit algorithm because all three algorithms make use of short-term memory.

The basic idea of QU-List is to perform Q-learning on a learned history space. The Q-function is therefore not defined on states, but on history lists. In contrast to the Identify&Exploit algorithm, the Q-function and the history space are learned simultaneously. After every n_{ref} sampled transition instances, the history space is refined according to a reward-based criterion. The refinement process is adopted from the U-tree algorithm described in section 4.1.2. Detailed pseudocode of the refinement process is shown in Algorithm 8.

The complete QU-List algorithm is stated in Algorithm 9. A history list is

Maze	State Space ($|S|$)	Sarsa(λ)	% Optimal
Small	20	8.93	15 %
Big	104	155.85	45 %

Table 4.5: Average performance of policies learned by Sarsa(λ). The third column gives the number of steps to the goal averaged over every possible starting state. The fourth column gives the percentage of the twenty runs of Sarsa(λ), in which the optimal memoryless policy was found. An episode for testing the learned policy is aborted if the goal state is not reached after at most 200 steps.

extended at the front only if the Q-values of the extended list are significantly different from the original list. Since the Q-values correspond to the cumulative reward, the refinement process is guided by a reward-based criterion. The idea of this criterion is to build a history space such that it is possible to learn policies achieving a high cumulative reward. Note that there is no theoretical guarantee that Algorithm 8 is able to build such desirable history spaces.

The most important parameters of the complete QU-list algorithm (Algorithm 9) are the constant exploration rate ϵ, the constant learning rate α, the maximal number of iterations of the update loop N_{max}, and the frequency n_{ref} of refinement steps. In contrast to the Identify&Exploit algorithm, the Q-learning updates performed by QU-list do not necessarily converge to a fixed point. Thus, by introducing the parameter N_{max}, we stop the Q-learning update loop after a fixed number of iterations of the loop. To increase the likelihood that Q-learning still converges, the QU-list algorithm uses a constant learning rate $\alpha < 1$. Although not explicitly stated in the pseudocode, the Algorithm 8 is called several times in a row to make the refinement process more efficient.

The QU-list algorithm differs from the original implementation of U-tree in several ways. However, we are confident that QU-list is at least equally powerful, since we successfully used parts of the QU-list algorithm in our own algorithms[3]. The extensions implemented for QU-list were developed in order to solve problems we encountered while using U-tree. It follows a summary of the main differences of the QU-list algorithm compared to the original implementation of U-tree from [McC95].

1. Instead of using decision trees, QU-list represents short-term memory in the form of history lists. This should not make a difference with respect to the quality of the policies learned, since the two representations are almost equivalent. Note that a decision tree containing sequences of observations and actions can be easily decomposed into a set of history lists (Figure 4.1). We found history lists to be more practical, since we already developed a framework for history lists.

2. Instead of learning a model from sampled transition instances and then applying value iteration, QU-list uses a variant of Q-learning to derive a

---
[3] In the next section we will present an algorithm sharing ideas with the QU-list algorithm.

Algorithm 8 Refinement of History Space
―――
1: Build all one-step extensions (at the front) of all history lists in H and add the new history lists to a candidate set H_c. One step means a single action-observation pair. Only those extensions are considered which actually occur on sampled episodes from $\mathcal{F}$
2: Build a set of candidate transitions $\mathcal{F}_c^h$ for every candidate list $h \in H_c$. The set $\mathcal{F}_c^h$ is derived from the original set of transitions $\mathcal{F}$ by recomputing, for every episode $\mathcal{E} = [a_0, o_0, ..., a_{L-1}, o_L]$ from $\mathcal{F}$, the sequence of current history lists $\{h_t \mid (0 \leq t \leq L)\}$ based on an extended history space $H \cup \{h\}$. All resulting (recomputed) transition instances (h_t, a_t, r_t, h_{t+1}) in which history list h occurs are added to the set F_c^h
3: Consider the following sets of real numbers:

$$\forall h \in H, \forall a \in A : \hat{Q}_1^{h,a} := \{r + \beta \max_{a' \in A} \hat{Q}(h', a') \mid (h, a, r, h') \in \mathcal{F}\}$$

$$\forall h \in H_c, \forall a \in A : \hat{Q}_2^{h,a} := \{r + \beta \max_{a' \in A} \hat{Q}(h', a') \mid (h, a, r, h') \in \mathcal{F}_c^h\}$$

If $h_c \in H_c$ is a one-step extension of history list $h \in H$, the two sets $Q_1^{h,a}$ and $Q_2^{h_c,a}$ are compared by a statistical test (Kolmogorov-Smirnov) for all actions $a \in A$. If for an action $a \in A$, the set $Q_1^{h,a}$ is sampled from a different distribution than the set $Q_2^{h_c,a}$, then h_c is included into H. Otherwise, h_c is discarded
―――

policy. In [McC95], the author points out that Q-learning is a reasonable extension to the U-tree algorithm.

3. In order to speed up Q-learning, the QU-list algorithm performs batch updates of the Q-function by iterating over the set $\mathcal{F}$. This is much more efficient compared to ordinary Q-learning (Algorithm 1), since every sampled transition instance can be used several times.

4. To make QU-list applicable to large state spaces, we implemented a basic form of temporal abstraction which can be turned on or off according to the needs of the problem setting considered. The idea is to repeatedly execute the same action as long as the current observation does not change. This significantly reduces the total number of action choices and therefore simplifies the learning problem. A transition instance is created at time t only if $o_t \neq o_{t-1}$. The reward signal r_t is therefore the cumulative reward, since the last time a transition instance was created. The current history list h_t is computed based on this new shorter sequence of observations and actions. This can also be regarded as a simple form of options [SPS99]. In Figure 4.10, an example of an abstract transition is shown. To keep the pseudocode of the QU-list algorithm simple, temporal abstraction is not included into the definition of Algorithm 9.

We will now present an empirical evaluation of the QU-List algorithm by

Algorithm 9 QU-List
1: $\mathcal{F} \leftarrow \emptyset$
2: $H \leftarrow \{[ao] \mid a \in A, o \in O\}$
3: $\forall a \in A, \forall h \in H : \hat{Q}(h, a) \leftarrow 0$
4: **repeat**
5:   Sample a set of episodes consisting of transition instances $\mathcal{F}_{new}$ by an ϵ-greedy exploration strategy. The greedy actions are extracted from the approximated Q-function $\hat{Q}$
6:   $\mathcal{F} \leftarrow \mathcal{F} \cup \mathcal{F}_{new}$
7:   **for** $i = 0$ to N_{max} **do**
8:     **for all** $(h_t, a_t, r_t, h_{t+1}) \in \mathcal{F}$ **do**
9:       $\hat{Q}(h_t, a_t) \leftarrow (1 - \alpha)\hat{Q}(h_t, a_t) + \alpha(r_t + \beta \max_{a \in A} \hat{Q}(h_{t+1}, a))$
10:     **end for**
11:   **end for**
12:   After every n_{ref} sampled transition instances, call Algorithm 8 to refine the history space H
13: **until** the size of $\mathcal{F}$ exceeds a certain threshold

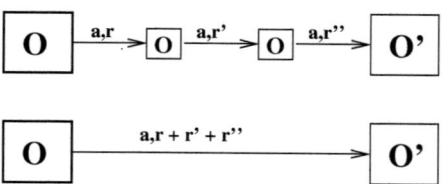

Figure 4.10: Three ordinary transitions compared to one abstract transition. Only a single abstract transition is created, because the first three observations of the sequence are all the same. The reward of the abstract transition equals the cumulative reward of the three single transitions. If temporal abstraction is used in such a manner, the current history list is derived from the new shorter sequence of observations and actions.

applying QU-list to both partially observable mazes. As summary of the performance of the QU-List algorithm is given in Table 4.6.

Maze	State Space	QU-List
Small	20	2.72
Big	104	31.26

Table 4.6: Average performance of policies learned by the QU-List algorithm. The third column gives the number of steps to the goal averaged over every possible starting state.

For the small maze, it was possible to learn surprisingly good policies. Temporal abstraction was disabled for this experiment. The experiment consists of twenty runs of the QU-list algorithm. A learning curve is shown in Figure 4.11. The final average performance of the policies learned by QU-list for the

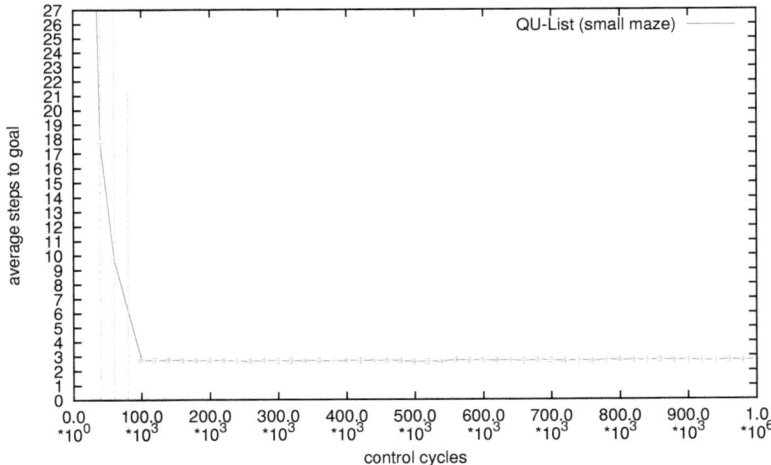

Figure 4.11: Policies learned for the small maze by the QU-list algorithm. The x-axis shows the number of control cycles, while the y-axis shows the average number of steps to the goal. The number of steps to the goal is averaged over all possible starting states. Setting of parameters: Learning rate $\alpha = 0.2$, constant exploration rate $\epsilon = 0.3$, discounting rate $\beta = 1$, $N_{max} = 200$ and $n_{ref} = 1000$ sampled transition instances.

small maze is an average number of 2.72 steps to the goal, which is very close to the optimal solution. The size of the history spaces built by QU-list is around $|H| = 1000$ with very small variance. Why is QU-list able to find such good policies?

The QU-list algorithm does not distinguish between identifying history lists and non-identifying history lists. A policy for a history list $h \in H$ is derived by extracting a greedy action from the learned Q-function, no matter if h identifies a state or not. For small state spaces, this heuristic works well because of the following reasons:

1. If the state space is small, short history lists suffice to identify the current state. Thus, most history lists from H identify a state anyway. The Q-learning updates are therefore likely to converge even if this is not guaranteed from a theoretical point of view. Also the statistical tests used by QU-list work reliably, since the approximated Q-function is relatively close to the actual cumulated rewards achieved.

2. If the small maze is considered, the Q-values provide a better heuristic for the selection of actions than an efficient identification strategy. This is due to the fact that identification steps become almost irrelevant if the goal is only a very few steps away. For the small maze, an efficient identification strategy causes unnecessary overhead.

We also tried to apply the QU-list algorithm to the big maze. Unfortunately, we were not able to learn successful policies at all. To find the goal state of the big maze, relatively long history lists are necessary. In other words, it is not possible to define good policies on short history lists. Since QU-list starts with history lists having a length of one, Q-learning is not able to compute meaningful Q-values for these lists. As a consequence, the statistical tests relying on the Q-values are not able to extend the lists in such a way that the resulting history space can be used to learn good policies. To summarize, the QU-list algorithm lacks theoretical guarantees with respect to the procedure of building a history space and learning policies on this space.

However, by making use of temporal abstraction as described above, the space of policies considered by QU-list can be significantly reduced. In Figure 4.12, we present results of ten runs of the QU-list algorithms applied to the big maze using temporal abstraction. The final average performance of the policies learned by the QU-list algorithm for the big maze is an average number of 31.26 steps to the goal. As can be seen from the learning curve, the learning process is somewhat unstable. Since average values are less meaningful for high variances, we summarized in Table 4.7 the best and the worst policy learned.

Maze	QU-List (average)	QU-List (best)	QU-List (worst)
Big	31.26	11.51	84.39

Table 4.7: Best and worst performance of policies for the big maze learned by the QU-list algorithm with temporal abstraction. The third column gives the performance of the best run, while the fourth column gives the performance of the worst run. The performance of a policy is expressed by the average number of steps to the goal.

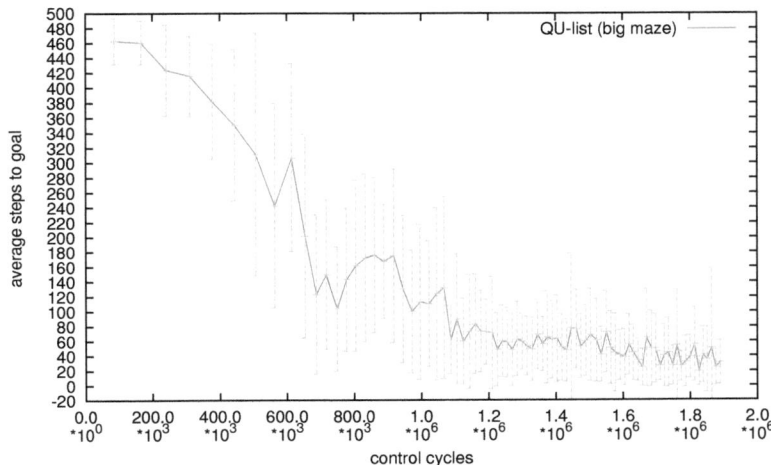

Figure 4.12: Policies learned for the big maze by the QU-list algorithm with temporal abstraction. The x-axis shows the number of control cycles, while the y-axis shows the average number of steps to the goal. The number of steps to the goal is averaged over all possible starting states. Setting of parameters: Learning rate $\alpha = 0.1$, constant exploration rate $\epsilon = 0.1$, discounting rate $\beta = 1$, $N_{max} = 200$ and $n_{ref} = 40$ sampled episodes.

The history spaces learned by QU-list were very small. All runs of QU-list learned a history space of size $400 \leq |H| \leq 1000$. This is due to the fact that temporal abstraction drastically reduces the length of the history lists used. An abstract episode is very short compared to an ordinary one, since the number of abstract transitions is much less than the number of ordinary transitions. Thus, if temporal abstraction is used, then short history lists suffice to define good policies. A history space H built by using temporal abstraction is therefore much smaller than a history space built without temporal abstraction.

Note that a temporarily abstract POMDP is different from the original POMDP considered. The optimal solution of the temporarily abstract POMDP is possibly worse than for the original one, since much information about the complete sequence of past observations is ignored. In other words, the space of policies available for temporarily abstract POMDPs is a subset of the space of policies available for the original POMDP. However, as discussed later, for continuous state space, it is inevitable to introduce some form of temporal abstraction.

Applying the Identify&Exploit Algorithm to Complete History Spaces

To give an impression of how much memory is generally necessary to define successful policies for the partially observable mazes, Table 4.8 provides the sufficient history lengths for these particular POMDPs. We computed the constants by a separate software tool we developed for analyzing history spaces for deterministic POMDPs.

Maze	State Space ($|S|$)	Sufficient History Length (l_{su})
Small	20	3
Big	104	5

Table 4.8: The sufficient history length of the partially observable mazes shown in Figure 4.4. The small maze consists of the lower right part of the original maze.

To analyze the performance of policies learned by the Identify&Exploit algorithm, we first built five different k-complete history spaces by the procedure stated in Algorithm 6. While only a single k-complete history space was built for the small maze ($k = 6$), four different types of history spaces were built for the big maze ($k \in \{6, 7, 8, 9\}$). A bit of prior knowledge is included in the learning process, since Algorithm 6 makes use of the correct sufficient history length l_{su}. However, as long as the sufficient history length is not underestimated, both Algorithm 6 as well as the Identify&Exploit algorithm also work reliably for a rough guess of the constant l_{su}.

How does a particular estimate of l_{su} affect the performance of Algorithm 6 for learning complete history spaces? The constant l_{su} determines how many front extensions of identifying history lists are excluded from the history space H. Since front extensions of identifying history lists are not necessary at all for building k-complete history spaces, it does not harm the quality of the learned spaces if l_{su} is overestimated. A problem occurs only if l_{su} is underestimated. In such a situation, too many front extensions of minimal identifying history lists are included into H preventing the algorithm from building a k-complete history space.

What about the Identify&Exploit algorithm? For our empirical evaluation of the Identify&Exploit algorithm, we used the correct values for l_{su}. The criterion CC for detecting identifying history lists is guaranteed to classify a list $h \in H$ perfectly if it holds that $|h| \leq k - l_{su}$ (Theorem 4). If l_{su} is overestimated, then criterion CC detects a lesser number of identifying history lists. If l_{su} is underestimated, criterion CC is not guaranteed to work correctly anymore, i.e some non-identifying history lists may be wrongly classified as identifying.

It is possible to interpret the empirical results for different estimates of the constant l_{su} by again considering the inequality $|h| \leq k - l_{su}$. For example, assume that a k-complete history space is available and the sufficient history length l_{su} is overestimated by $l_{su} + x$. Then, the resulting performance of criterion CC corresponds to the performance achieved for a $(k - x)$-complete history space using the correct sufficient history length l_{su}.

Learning Complete History Spaces for Partially Observable Mazes

In Table 4.9, the basic properties of the history spaces learned are summarized. The experiments of learning k-complete history spaces were repeated twenty times. We verified by using our software tool for analyzing history spaces, that all spaces learned were actually k-complete.

Maze	k	Size ($|H|$)	Detected Identifying Lists
Small	6	3511.2 (29.4)	2116.45 (16.6)
Big	6	55506.8 (139.4)	1 (0)
Big	7	137359.5 (333.1)	11502.9 (105.7)
Big	8	141514.5 (523.24)	10278.1 (119.8)
Big	9	288114.6 (583.2)	24866.5 (152)

Table 4.9: History spaces learned by Algorithm 6. The second column gives the parameter k of the algorithm. The third column gives the total size of the history space learned. The fourth column gives the number of identifying history lists from the learned space detected by criterion CC. All values shown are averaged over twenty runs. The numbers in braces give the standard deviation. All history spaces learned were actually k-complete.

To build the k-complete history spaces, Algorithm 6 collected a total number of $k*20000$ transition instances for the small maze and a total number of $k*200000$ transition instances for the big one. An exception is the 8-complete space, for which it surprisingly turned out that a number of $8*100000$ transition instances gave better results. This means that the Identify&Exploit algorithm was able to learn better policies on a smaller history space learned by sampling only $8*100000$ transition instances. The most likely explanation for this phenomenon is that sampling many instances causes Algorithm 6 to include many history lists into the history space. Since there exist many more non-identifying lists than identifying ones, most of the added lists are non-identifying. These non-identifying history lists are then used by the efficient identification strategy as intermediate steps on a path to an identifying history list. If many non-identifying history lists are available, then the identification strategy is able to find a path to an identifying history list having a very high probability of success. However, this is not always as desirable as it seems, because paths reaching an identifying history list with a very high probability of success are often very long and circuitous. A reasonable extension to our identification strategy would be therefore to select a path to an identifying history list not only based on success probabilities but also on the cumulative reward. As discussed earlier, we leave this issue out for future work.

Since it takes five steps ($l_{su} = 5$) to identify an arbitrary state of the big maze, criterion CC can detect only few identifying history lists if the parameter k takes on low values. For example, consider the case $k = 6$. Since $k - l_{su} = 6 - 5 = 1$, it follows from Theorem 4 that criterion CC is able to classify history lists having a length of at most one. It is easy to see that the only identifying history list of length one is the history list consisting of the goal observation. This is the reason why the second row of Table 4.9 states that there is only a single identifying history list detected by criterion CC.

Combining the Identify&Exploit Algorithm with Criterion CC

After having the history spaces learned, we employed the Safe Q-Learning algorithm (Algorithm 4) to learn a Q-function on these spaces. Remember that extensions of identifying history lists are again identifying (Lemma 4 and Lemma 5). Thus, we considered extensions (front or tail) of a history list $h \in H$ to be identifying if h is classified as identifying by criterion CC. It is easy to see that such a procedure does not harm the convergence proof for Q-learning (Theorem 5). History lists which do not satisfy the assumptions made by Theorem 4 are classified as non-identifying by criterion CC.

To point out the importance of the efficient identification strategy, we repeated all learning experiments with a random identification. The random identification chooses an action at random if the current history list is non-identifying. Otherwise, a greedy action is extracted from the Q-function.

To find an optimal set of parameters, we performed a coarse search in the parameter space before starting the final experiments. In Figure 4.13, the performance of policies learned for the small maze is shown. For each of the twenty history spaces built, a Q-function was learned by a separate run of the Safe Q-Learning algorithm. The learned Q-function was tested by applying the Identify&Exploit algorithm (Algorithm 3).

Figure 4.14 show analogous results for the 9-complete history spaces built for the big maze. Individual learning curves for the other history spaces ($k \in \{6, 7, 8\}$) can be found in the appendix. To show that the performance of policies increases with the parameter k, i.e. with the amount of memory used, we replotted all learning curves for the big maze in Figure 4.15. Note that Figure 4.15 shows the complete learning curves ($4*10^6$ control cycles), while the Figures 4.13 and 4.14 show only the most important parts of the learning curves ($2*10^6$ control cycles). The learning curves presented show average values over twenty runs supplemented by the standard deviation.

To summarize the results of the experiments, Table 4.10 shows the performance of all final policies learned. The values are again averaged over twenty runs of the algorithm.

From the Figures 4.13 and 4.14, it can be seen that the efficient identification strategy yields much better results than the random identification strategy. Except for the 6-complete history space, the Identify&Exploit algorithm converges smoothly to a final policy. The performance of the policies learned is reasonably close to the optimal policies. The worse results for the 6-complete history space are caused by the fact that criterion CC is applicable only to a single history list (Table 4.9). Thus, for the 6-complete history space, almost all his-

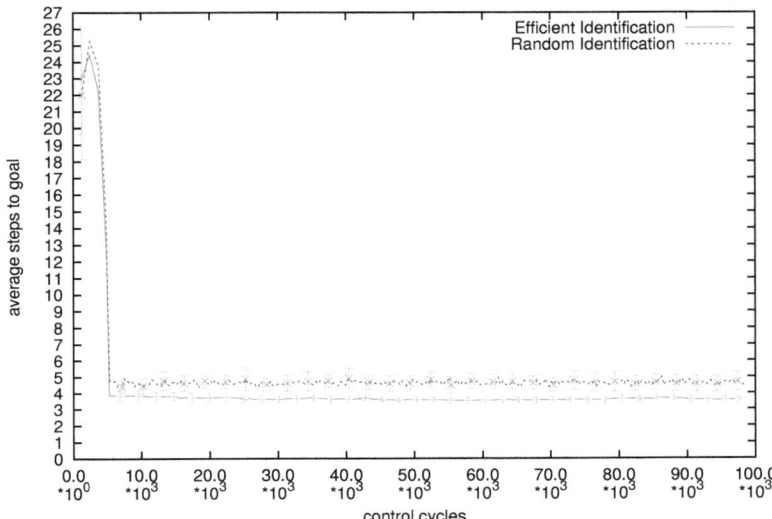

Figure 4.13: The Identify&Exploit algorithm applied to the small maze using criterion CC. The x-axis shows the number of control cycles, while the y-axis shows the number of steps to the goal averaged over all possible starting states. Setting of parameters: 6-complete history space, constant exploration rate $\epsilon = 0.1$, discounting rate $\beta = 1.0$, and the maximal search depth $L = 2$ (efficient identification). After every $|\mathcal{F}_{new}| = 5000$ sampled transition instances, the Q-learning update loop was executed.

tory lists are classified as non-identifying and the Identify&Exploit algorithm becomes equivalent to a search prodcedure consisting of the efficient identification strategy. However, the results show that dividing the overall problem into an identification phase and an exploitation phase works well for the mazes considered.

Another interesting observation we made is that for low values of k, a deeper search for identifying history lists is necessary than for high values of k. The search depth is given by the parameter L. This phenomenon can be explained by the fact that for high values of k, criterion CC is able to detect many identifying history lists (Table 4.9). Thus, if many identifying history lists are available, the efficient identification strategy may find a path to an identifying history list very easily.

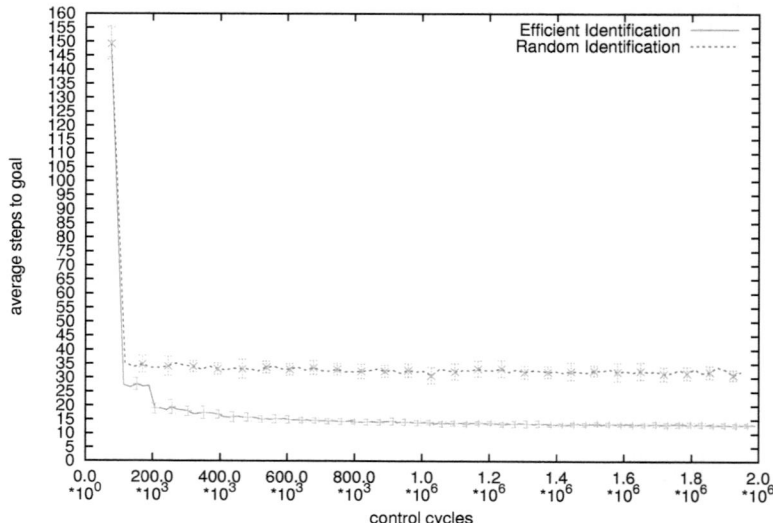

Figure 4.14: The Identify&Exploit algorithm applied to the big maze using criterion CC. The x-axis shows the number of control cycles, while the y-axis shows the number of steps to the goal averaged over all possible starting states. Setting of parameters: 9-complete history space, constant exploration rate $\epsilon = 0.2$, discounting rate $\beta = 1.0$, and the maximal search depth $L = 2$ (efficient identification). After every $|\mathcal{F}_{new}| = 100000$ sampled transition instances, the Q-learning update loop was executed.

Maze	k	Search Depth (L)	Identify&Exploit
Small	6	2	3.56
Big	6	7	32.47
Big	7	4	16.71
Big	8	3	15.45
Big	9	2	12.80

Table 4.10: Performance of the Identify&Exploit algorithm using criterion CC for detecting identifying history lists. The second column shows the type of history space and the third column shows the maximal search depth used by the efficient identification strategy. The fourth column shows the number of steps to the goal averaged over all possible starting states.

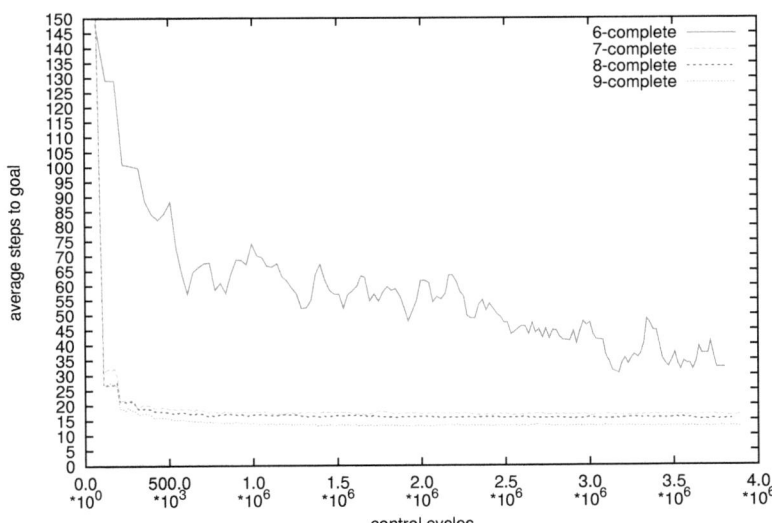

Figure 4.15: The Identify&Exploit algorithm applied to the big maze using the efficient identification strategy and criterion CC. The x-axis shows the number of control cycles, while the y-axis shows the number of steps to the goal averaged over all possible starting states.

4.3 Scaling Up the Identify&Exploit Algorithm

The theoretical and empirical results presented so far show that it is promising to apply the Identify&Exploit algorithm to k-complete history spaces. However, if the state space is infinite, a k-complete history space does not provide enough information about past events to perfectly identify every single state.

Lemma 8. *Sufficient History Length for Infinite State Spaces*
Let $M := (T, S, A, O, f_S, f_O, r)$ be a deterministic POMDP such that S is an infinite set of states and O is a finite set of observations. Then, it holds that $l_{su} = \infty$.

The proof of Lemma 8 can be found in the appendix. Given an infinite state space, using a k-complete history space may be impractical for several reasons.

- If the state space is of infinite size, the sufficient history length l_{su} is infinite as well. In such a setting, criterion CC is not able to detect a single identifying history list, even if a k-complete history space is available (Theorem 4). The applicability of criterion CC is therefore limited to finite state spaces.

- In the worst case, the size of a k-complete space grows exponentially in the parameter k. Learning k-complete history spaces is practical only for problems which can be solved with reasonably little memory.

- For learning a k-complete history space, it is necessary to sample a set of transition instances $\mathcal{F}$. In order to avoid a high sample complexity, it may be desirable to define policies also on "incomplete" history spaces.

To solve the problems mentioned above, we will present an alternative criterion for detecting identifying history lists. This criterion can be applied both to arbitrary history spaces as well as to arbitrary state spaces without destroying convergence of the Safe Q-Learning algorithm. However, the theoretical guarantees with respect to the performance of the new criterion will be somewhat weaker than for criterion CC.

4.3.1 An Alternative Criterion for Detecting Identifying History Lists

Definition 25. *Criterion for Detecting Identifying History Lists (CE)*
Let $H \subset H^*$ be a history space. A history list $h \in H$ is called identifying according to criterion CE and a set of transition instances $\mathcal{F}$ if the following condition is satisfied for every pair of transition instances from $\mathcal{F}$:
$(h, a, r', h') \in \mathcal{F} \land (h, a, r'', h'') \in \mathcal{F} \Rightarrow r' = r'' \land h' = h''$.
We say that two transitions are conflicting if $r' \neq r''$ or $h' \neq h''$.

In contrast to criterion CC, criterion CE is based on empirical evidence in the form of sampled transition instances. Thus, it is not possible to analytically prove that criterion CE will classify every history list correctly. However, since we consider only deterministic POMDPs, we can prove some basic properties of criterion CE.

Lemma 9. *Detection of Identifying History Lists with Criterion CE*
Let $H \subset H^*$ be a history space. If a history list $h \in H$ is identifying a single state, then criterion CE will classify h correctly. Secondly, if $h \in H$ is non-identifying according to criterion CE, then h is actually not identifying a single state.

Proof. Consider two transition instances $(h, a, r', h') \in \mathcal{F}$, $(h, a, r'', h'') \in \mathcal{F}$. Assume that the first transition was sampled at time t and the second transition was sampled at time t'. Thus, it must hold that $h_t = h_{t'} = h$. If h is identifying a single state $s^h \in S$, it must hold that $s_t = s_{t'} = s^h$. If an action $a \in A$ is executed, then it holds that $s' := s_{t+1} = s_{t'+1} = f_S(s^h, a)$ and $o' := o_{t+1} = o_{t'+1} = f_O(s', a)$. It follows that the next current history lists $h_{t+1} = h'$ and $h_{t'+1} = h''$ are computed based on the same sequence of observations and actions. This sequence is given by $[h, a, o']$. It follows that $h' = h''$. Also the reward signals $r' = r'' = r(s^h, a)$ must be the same. The condition stated in the definition of criterion CE is therefore satisfied and h is classified as an identifying history list.

We now assume that there are conflicting transitions in $\mathcal{F}$ such that $(h, a, r', h') \in \mathcal{F}$ and $(h, a, r'', h'') \in \mathcal{F}$ with $r' \neq r''$ or $h' \neq h''$. If $r' \neq r''$, the states of the process before executing action $a \in A$ must have been different for the two transitions, since the reward function r is deterministic. Thus, h is not identifying a single state. Similarly, if $h' \neq h''$, the observations made after executing $a \in A$ must have been different for the two transitions, since the observation model f_O is deterministic. Thus, the states of the process before executing action $a \in A$ must have been different. Thus, h cannot be identifying for a single state. □

There are only a few situations in which criterion CE fails to classify a history list $h \in H$ correctly. For such a situation to occur, it must be the case that h is non-identifying and there are no conflicting transition instances for h in $\mathcal{F}$. A reasonable solution to this problem is to increase the number of sampled transition instances. We will later discuss some other practical methods for increasing the accuracy of criterion CE.

How is the performance of the Identify&Exploit algorithm affected by the use of criterion CE? Like for criterion CC, we can show that the Identify&Exploit algorithm is sound in the sense that Q-learning converges to a unique fixed point.

Theorem 6. *Convergence of Q-Learning on Arbitrary History Spaces*
Let $M := (T, S, A, O, f_S, f_O, r)$ be a deterministic partially observable Markov decision process. Let $0 \leq \beta < 1$ be a discounting rate and let $H \subset H^*$ be a history space. If criterion CE is used to detect identifying history lists and the state space S is finite, then the Safe Q-Learning algorithm (Algorithm 4) will

converge to a unique Q-function. If the state space S is infinite, then for every single run of the Q-learning update loop of the Safe Q-Learning algorithm, the Q-function converges to a unique fixed point. In both cases, there exists a deterministic MDP M_H such that the greedy policy extracted from the approximated Q-function constitutes an optimal policy for M_H.

Proof. The proof is an adaptation of the proof for Theorem 5. A deterministic MDP M_H will be created such that all Q-learning updates performed by the Safe Q-Learning algorithm are equivalent to ordinary Q-learning updates on the MDP M_H.

If the state space is finite, the same arguments as in the proof for Theorem 5 can be used to show that the set of transitions $\mathcal{F}$ converges to a final set $\mathcal{F}_\infty$. If the state space is infinite, then we consider only a single run of the Q-learning update loop, given a set of sampled transitions $\mathcal{F}$. Since the process of creating a deterministic MDP M_H from the set $\mathcal{F}_\infty$ is equivalent to the process of creating a deterministic MDP M_H from the set $\mathcal{F}$, we will show the proof only once using the set $\mathcal{F}_\infty$.

We will now discuss the individual components of the constructed MDP $M_H := (T_H, S_H, A_H, f_H, r_H)$ based on the final set of transition instances $\mathcal{F}_\infty$. In the following, the set $\mathcal{F}^{vl}$ denotes the set of valid transitions derived from the set $\mathcal{F}_\infty$.

Time Steps The set of time steps is adopted from the POMDP M ($T_H := T$)

State Space The state space of M_H consists of a set of history lists $S_H \subseteq H$. Stated precisely, S_H contains all history lists $h \in H$ classified as identifying according to criterion CE and the set of transitions $\mathcal{F}_\infty$.

Actions The actions are adopted from the POMDP M ($A_H := A$). However, the set of actions executable from a history list $h \in S_H$ is restricted to the set $A_h^{vl} \subseteq A$. In subsection 4.2.3, a procedure is given to compute the set A_h^{vl} from the final set of sampled transition instances $\mathcal{F}_\infty$.

Transition Model The transition model is deterministic and can therefore be represented by a function $f_H : S_H \times A \to S_H$. We define $f_H(h, a) := h'$ for history lists $h \in S_H, h' \in S_H$ and an action $a \in A_h^{vl}$ if there exists a transition instance $(h_t = h, a_t = a, r_t = r', h_{t+1} = h') \in \mathcal{F}^{vl}$. From the definition of the set A_h^{vl}, it follows that there exists at least one such transition instance with $h \in S_H$.

It remains to show that f_H is well-defined and $h' \in S_H$. We assume a sampled transition instance $(h_t = h, a_t = a, r_t = r', h_{t+1} = h') \in \mathcal{F}^{vl}$ generated by the transition model f_S and the observation model f_O. Since $h \in S_H$ is identifying according to criterion CE and the set $\mathcal{F}_\infty$, it follows that for every other transition $(h_t = h, a_t = a, r_t = r'', h_{t+1} = h'') \in \mathcal{F}^{vl} \subseteq \mathcal{F}_\infty$ that it holds $h' = h''$ and $r' = r''$. Thus, the transition function f_H is well-defined.

It also holds that $h' \in S_H$. Since $(h_t = h, a_t = a, r_t = r', h_{t+1} = h') \in \mathcal{F}^{vl}$ and we have shown that $h' \in H$ is the unique successor list of $h \in H$ after executing $a \in A_h^{vl}$, it must hold that $h' \in S_H$ by the definition of the set A_h^{vl}.

Reward Function The reward function $r_H : S_H \times A \to \mathbb{R}$ is defined as $r_H(h, a) := r'$ if there exists a transition instance $(h_t = h, a_t = a, r_t = r', h_{t+1} = h') \in \mathcal{F}^{vl}$. With the same arguments as for the transition model, we conclude that the reward function r_H is well-defined.

Since both functions f_H and r_H are deterministic, the process M_H is a deterministic Markov decision process (MDP). We will show that the Q-learning updates performed by Algorithm 4 are equivalent to ordinary Q-learning updates on M_H. An ordinary Q-learning update is defined in Algorithm 1 ($\alpha = 1$).
($\Rightarrow$): Assume that an update is made by Algorithm 4 for a transition instance $(h_t = h, a_t = a, r_t = r', h_{t+1} = h') \in \mathcal{F}^{vl}$. It immediately follows from the definition of Algorithm 4 that $a \in A_h^{vl}$ and $h' \in S_H$. From the definition of the set A_h^{vl}, it also follows that $h \in S_H$. Since h is identifying according to criterion CE and the set of valid transitions $\mathcal{F}^{vl}$, it holds that the reward signal $r_t = r'$ and the successor list $h_{t+1} = h'$ from a sampled transition are uniquely determined given the history list $h_t = h$ and action $a_t = a$. From the definition of the constructed MDP M_H it then follows that $f_H(h, a) = h'$ and $r_H(h, a) = r'$. Thus, the update performed by Algorithm 4 is an ordinary Q-learning update on MDP M_H.
($\Leftarrow$): Assume a history list $h \in S_H$ and an action $a \in A_h^{vl}$ such that $h' := f_H(h, a)$ and $r' := r_H(h, a)$. These are the components of an ordinary Q-learning update for MDP M_H. It follows from the definition of the transition model f_H that there exists a transition instance $\mathcal{T} := (h_t = h, a_t = a, r_t = r', h_{t+1} = h') \in \mathcal{F}^{vl}$. Thus, an ordinary Q-learning update on MDP M_H is performed by Algorithm 4 for transition $\mathcal{T}$.

The rest of the proof follows with the same arguments as given in the proof for Theorem 5. □

Discussion and Tuning of Criterion CE

Before applying criterion CE to the maze benchmark, we want to discuss what results we can expect based on the analysis presented so far. The convergence proof with respect to criterion CE (Theorem 6) holds for arbitrary history spaces as well as for arbitrary state spaces. However, if the state space is infinite, convergence is restricted to single runs of the Q-learning update loop. Note that the proof does not make use of the fact that the POMDPs considered are deterministic.

The basic idea of criterion CE is rather simple. Those history lists in H from which non-deterministic transitions to other history lists occur, are classified as non-identifying. These lists are excluded from updating the Q-function. In other words, a history list $h \in H$ is used for Q-learning only if there is empirical evidence that h identifies a state.

Given an identifying history list, we know from Lemma 9 that criterion CE will correctly classify the list. This assertion also holds for criterion CC, if the history space H used is k-complete (Theorem 4). We conclude that criterion CE detects at least as many identifying history lists as criterion CC will do. In fact, criterion CE detects many more identifying history lists, since criterion CC is applied only on the subset $\{h \in H \mid |h| \leq k - l_{su}\} \subseteq H$ of the history space.

A shortcoming of criterion CE is that some non-identifying history lists may be wrongly classified as identifying history lists. Since criterion CE is based on empirical evidence, the accuracy of the criterion strongly depends on the set of sampled transition instances $\mathcal{F}$. This does not harm the convergence of Q-learning, but it may influence the performance of the policies learned. The Q-values computed for wrongly classified history lists are not necessarily meaningful and the efficient identification strategy is less likely to find an action sequence to an identifying history list. Fortunately, this problem is not very serious for short history lists. A short history list frequently appears on sampled episodes. Since there is much empirical evidence available for such a history list, it is unlikely that the list will be wrongly classified by criterion CE. However, a long history list possibly occurs only a few times on sampled episodes, and conflicting transition instances are therefore hard to find for such a list. We tackle this problem by classifying a long history list as identifying only if the list is an extension of a shorter, already detected identifying history list (Lemma 4 and Lemma 5). In particular, for the maze benchmark, we consider a history list of a 6-complete (7,8,9-complete) history space to be long if it contains more than 3 (4,4,5) observations. These thresholds are derived from preliminary experiments. Unfortunately, some identifying history lists, which are not extensions of shorter identifying history list, will be wrongly classified as non-identifying by this procedure. Note that this kind of tuning does not invalidate the results from Theorem 6 and Lemma 9.

Another concern with respect to criterion CE is that to reliably detect non-identifying history lists, it may be necessary to consider n-step successors instead of the direct (one step) successors. For example, consider a sequence of two actions a, a' starting from a non-identifying history list h. Even if action a always leads to the same one-step successor $h' \in H$, the two-step successor $h'' \in H$ may be ambiguous after executing action a'. History list h will be wrongly classified as identifying, because criterion CE considers only one-step successors. We tackle this problem by improving criterion CE in the following way: We know from the Lemmas 4 and 5 that extensions of identifying history lists are again identifying. Similarly, it is easy to prove that a suffix of a non-identifying history list is also non-identifying. For example, if a long history list $h \in H$ is classified as non-identifying by criterion CE, then every shorter history list $h' \in H$ constituting a suffix of h must be non-identifying as well. By using this additional lemma, we can reduce the percentage of misclassified history lists due to ambiguous n-step successors. It would also be possible to detect ambiguous n-step successors by generalizing the definition of criterion CE. However, we decided to keep criterion CE as simple as possible.

- If criterion CE is generalized to n-step successors, it is not clear how to choose the parameter n.

- The computational effort of checking criterion CE for a history list $h \in H$ is minimized if only one-step successors are considered.

- If the history space H contains only very few identifying history lists, it may be desirable to compute Q-values for some non-identifying history lists as well. Paradoxically, failures of criterion CE are advantageous in these cases. In the next section, we will discuss this issue in more detail.

To illustrate the performance of criterion CE, we conducted additional experiments in which we sampled $2 * 10^6$ transitions using the Safe Q-Learning algorithm and then measured the number of correctly classified history lists. The 6-complete history spaces we used for these experiments were learned by the same setting of parameters as for the experiments for criterion CC.

Size ($|H|$)	Accuracy Ident.(%)	Accuracy Non-Ident.(%)
55478 (162)	83.5 (1)	100 (0)

Table 4.11: Performance of criterion CE on a 6-complete history space. The first column gives the size of the history space learned. The second column gives the percentage of correctly classified identifying history lists and the third column gives the percentage of correctly classified non-identifying history lists. All values are averaged over ten runs of the algorithm. The values given in braces denote the standard deviation.

We conclude that there is a trade-off between criterion CC and criterion CE. While criterion CC is applicable only to a restricted class of history spaces, it enables the Identify&Exploit algorithm to perfectly detect identifying history lists. In contrast to criterion CC, criterion CE works without any assumptions, but may cause a decrease in performance. From Table 4.11, we can see that criterion CE perfectly classifies non-identifying history lists while making some failures for identifying history lists. The tuning we implemented helped considerably to increase the accuracy of detecting non-identifying history lists. Unfortunately, as a side effect, this tuning caused a decrease of accuracy of detecting identifying history lists.

Applying Criterion CE to Complete History Spaces

For a direct comparison of criterion CC to criterion CE, we repeated the maze experiments presented in the last subsection, but using criterion CE for detecting identifying history lists. Again, we learned four different types of k-complete history spaces corresponding to different values of the parameter $k \in \{6, 7, 8, 9\}$. For applying the Safe Q-Learning algorithm to these spaces, we performed a coarse search for optimal parameter settings.

It turned out that discounting was necessary to make Q-learning converge. This is probably due to the fact that in contrast to criterion CC, criterion CE misclassifies some history lists. Thus, the history list MDP constructed in the proof for Theorem 6 does not satisfy all assumptions needed for guaranteeing convergence also for the undiscounted case.

We considered only the big maze for which we used only the efficient identification strategy. Figure 4.16 shows results for the 9-complete history space. Individual learning curves for the other history spaces can be found in the appendix.

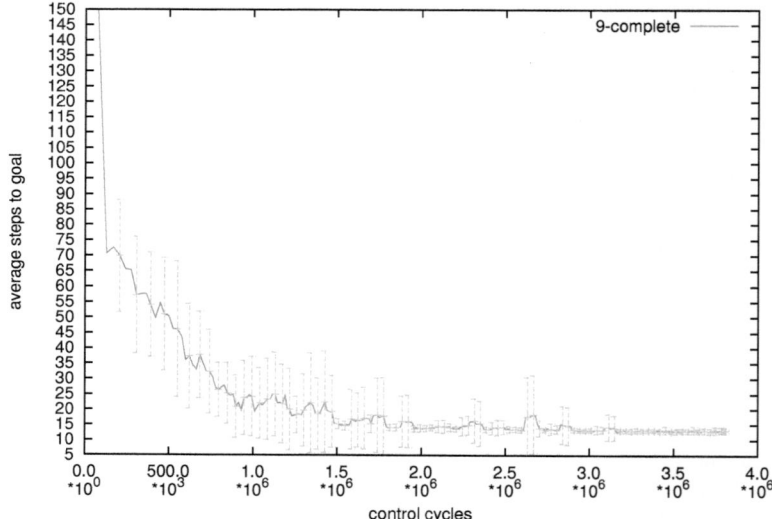

Figure 4.16: The Identify&Exploit algorithm applied to the big maze using criterion CE. The x-axis shows the number of control cycles, while the y-axis shows the number of steps to the goal averaged over all possible starting states. Setting of parameters: 9-complete history space, constant exploration rate $\epsilon = 0.2$, discounting rate $\beta = 0.98$, and the maximal search depth $L = 2$ (efficient identification). After every $|\mathcal{F}| = 100000$ sampled transition instances, the Q-learning update loop was executed.

To illustrate the different performances achieved for different history spaces, Figure 4.17 shows all learning curves within a single diagram. All values presented in Figures 4.16 and 4.17 are averaged over twenty runs of the algorithm. To enable a better comparison to criterion CC, we summarized the performances of the final policies learned in Table 4.12.

Interestingly, the performance of criterion CE is very similar to the performance of criterion CC, except for $k = 6$. Since criterion CE can be applied to all

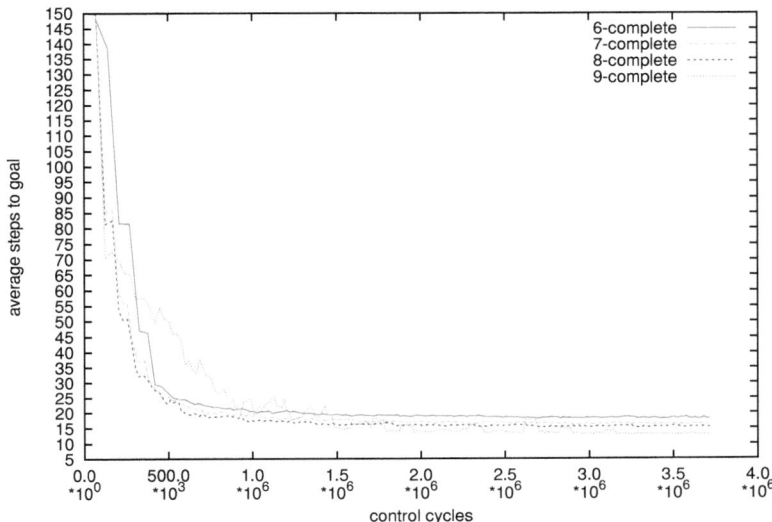

Figure 4.17: The Identify&Exploit algorithm applied to the big maze using the efficient identification strategy and criterion CE. The x-axis shows the number of control cycles, while the y-axis shows the number of steps to the goal averaged over all possible starting states.

history lists of the learned history space, good results can be achieved even for the smallest (6-complete) history space. As for criterion CC, the performance of the policies increases monotonically with the length of the history lists used.

To show the robustness of criterion CE, we randomly deleted a constant number of history lists from the 6-complete history spaces learned and then applied the Identify&Exploit algorithm to the resulting incomplete history spaces. The setting of parameters was unchanged. Table 4.13 shows the performance of the final policies learned.

If too many history lists are deleted from the 6-complete history spaces, the learning process becomes unstable. This fact is reflected by the high variance of the final performance. While some runs of the algorithm still yield very good policies, other runs converged to very bad policies. Most important for learning successful policies are the short history lists, which are easy to classify by criterion CE. It turned out that removing very long history lists from the history space had little effect on the final performance. However, if not enough short history lists are present in the history space, the performance decreases dramatically. Intuitively, short history lists constitute the backbone of the history space, while long history lists can be regarded as extensions allowing the performance to be tuned.

Maze	k	Criterion CE	Criterion CC
Big	6	18.25	32.47
Big	7	16.41	16.71
Big	8	15.35	15.45
Big	9	13.19	12.8

Table 4.12: Performance of the Identify&Exploit algorithm using criterion CE for detecting identifying history lists. The second column shows the type of history space used. The third column shows the number of steps to the goal averaged over all possible starting states for criterion CE. The fourth column shows the corresponding performance of criterion CC.

Size ($|H|$)	# Deleted Lists	Criterion CE
55478 (162)	1000	18.13 (0.87)
55478 (162)	5000	35.72 (30.28)
55478 (162)	10000	38.94 (29.9)

Table 4.13: Performance of the Identify&Exploit algorithm using criterion CE on incomplete history spaces. The first column shows the size of the learned history spaces. For all three experiments, the same history spaces were used. The second column shows the number of randomly deleted history lists and the third column shows the performance of the final policies learned. All values are averaged over ten runs of the algorithm. The values given in braces denote the standard deviation.

We conclude that criterion CE is more practical than criterion CC, since criterion CE works well with less memory and less assumptions concerning the history space and the state space. However, the benefits of criterion CC are that it has desirable theoretical properties and no tuning is necessary to learn good policies.

4.3.2 Abstract States with History

We now come back to the idea of creating an abstract state space by building sequences of past observations and actions, as discussed in the last chapter. In fact, the abstract state spaces considered in this section constitute a special type of history spaces. This can be illustrated by assuming a fully observable Markov decision process (MDP) with an infinite, continuous state space S. The basic idea for solving such a large MDP is to transform it into a POMDP and then apply the Identify&Exploit algorithm. The transformation is done by a well known technique for dealing with large state spaces: A feature vector is extracted from every state from S. The components (features) of this vector are finite valued, i.e. every component takes on values from a finite domain. What makes a feature vector interesting is the fact that features can be interpreted as observations of a state. A POMDP is built from the original MDP by defining the observation space O to be the finite set of all possible feature vectors. The observation of a state is therefore equivalent to the feature vector of this state. The benefit of using the Identify&Exploit algorithm to solve the resulting POMDP is that the learning agent processes only a finite number of abstract states instead of an infinite number of single states. An abstract state is given by a history list consisting of observations (feature vectors) and actions.

In the following, we will present empirical results for continuous MDPs which have been coarsely discretized. This can be interpreted as observing the current state at a coarser granularity. The loss of precision is compensated by building history lists. In such a setting, the discrete cells laid over the state space constitute the observations made by the agent. The only feature of a state is the cell index in which the state is falling. History lists are therefore sequences of cell indices and actions. What makes this approach especially appealing is the fact that ordinary Q-learning possibly diverges on a discretized state space. However, if the Identify&Exploit algorithm is combined with criterion CE, convergence of Q-learning is ensured by Theorem 6.

How to Use Criterion CE on Abstract State Spaces

If the state space S is continuous, the problem of learning good policies is much more complicated, since most single states cannot be identified by a history list of finite length. However, even if criterion CE is not able to detect identifying history lists for single states, it may still be able to detect identifying history lists for sets of states. Remember that identifying history lists are originally defined with respect to a subset $S' \subseteq S$ (Definition 19). In Figure 3.3, history lists identifying subsets of the state space are illustrated. If criterion CE is used to detect such lists, we can give an alternative interpretation of what it means to identify a set of states. Consider a history list $h \in H$ identifying a subset $S' \subseteq S$. Since the definition of criterion CE consists of conditioning future observations and rewards, the states belonging to the set S' are similar with respect to the observations and rewards that follow these states. In other words, the observation models of these states are similar or almost equivalent. The motivation for defining a policy on the history list h is to execute the same action at all states from S'. Theorem 6 guarantees that it is possible to learn a policy for h in a "safe" way. Here, safe means to preserve convergence of the Q-learning algorithm.

Unfortunately, from preliminary experiments we found out that for the benchmark problems we considered, almost all history lists were classified as non-identifying by criterion CE. Thus, we could compute Q-values only for a small number of history lists. We think the main reason for this sobering result is that criterion CE is not able to separate sets of similar states with high precision. To clarify this, consider once again the definition of criterion CE. A single transition instance conflicting with another sampled instance will force criterion CE to classify the corresponding history list as non-identifying. Thus, only very few history lists will be classified as identifying. We will therefore generalize criterion CE to a confidence parameter $0 \leq \delta \leq 1$.

Note that a set of transition instances $\mathcal{F}$ is not able to represent doubles of transitions, i.e. a transition occuring several times. Without loss of generality, we therefore consider the set $\mathcal{F}$ to be sampled from a single, very long episode. Every transition instance from $\mathcal{F}$ can therefore be indexed by a uniqe timestamp.

Definition 26. *Criterion for Detecting Identifying History Lists CE(δ)*
Let $H \subset H^*$ be a history space. Let $\delta \in \mathbb{R}$ be a constant from the closed interval $[0,1]$. A history list $h \in H$ is called identifying according to criterion CE(δ) and a set of transition instances $\mathcal{F}$ if the following condition is satisfied:
$$\forall a \in A,\ \exists h' \in H,\ \exists r' \in \mathbb{R}:\ \frac{|\{(h_t,a_t,r_t,h_{t+1}) \in \mathcal{F} \mid h_t=h, a_t=a, r_t=r', h_{t+1}=h'\}|}{|\{(h_t,a_t,r_t,h_{t+1}) \in \mathcal{F} \mid h_t=h, a_t=a\}|} \geq \delta$$

Choosing a particular value for δ enables to classify a history list as identifying, even if there are some conflicting transition instances stored in $\mathcal{F}$. These conflicts are simply ignored by criterion CE(δ). If $\delta = 0$, every history list is classified as identifying. If $\delta = 1$, criterion CE(δ) becomes equivalent to the strict version of criterion CE (Definition 25).

If δ is close to one, then a history list is classified as identifying by criterion CE(δ), only if h identifies a small subset of states. This is due to the fact that for high values of δ, the set of possible future observations and rewards of a history list classified as identifying by criterion CE(δ) must be very small. Thus, it is likely that there are only a few current states possible given that history list h becomes the current history list. These states are identified by history list h. Conversely, if δ takes on low values, history lists classified as identifying by criterion CE(δ) identify a possibly large set of states.

Unfortunately, if criterion CE(δ) is used for detecting identifying history lists, then the Safe Q-Learning algorithm is no longer guaranteed to converge to a unique Q-function. This is due to the fact that criterion CE(δ) allows Q-learning updates for conflicting transition instances. We therefore provide empirical results both for criterion CE(δ) as well as for a simple heuristic regaining the desirable convergence property. We call it the MaxProb heuristic and it works as follows: A transition instance $(h, a, r', h') \in \mathcal{F}$ is used for updating the Q-function at pair $(h, a) \in H \times A$, only if h' is the most probable successor list after executing action a in h. Stated precisely, the only transition instance used for updating the Q-function at pair $(h, a) \in H \times A$, is the instance $(h, a, r', h') \in \mathcal{F}$, maximizing δ from the expression $\frac{|\{(h_t,a_t,r_t,h_{t+1}) \in \mathcal{F} \mid h_t=h, a_t=a, r_t=r', h_{t+1}=h'\}|}{|\{(h_t,a_t,r_t,h_{t+1}) \in \mathcal{F} \mid h_t=h, a_t=a\}|} \geq \delta$. The MaxProb heuristic selects a transition instance serving as a good representative of the process. For example, if an action leads to a certain successor list with 95% probability, we ignore all other cases occurring with only 5% probability. Moreover, the heuristic can be derived from the definition of criterion CE(δ). More details concerning the MaxProb heuristic and how it is integrated into the Identify&Exploit algorithm follow in the next subsections.

Learning Abstract State Spaces with History

Similar to the discrete maze problems analyzed in the last section, a procedure is needed for learning a history space of high quality. Given the observations to be features of a state, history lists of these observations must be learned such that near optimal policies can be defined on the resulting history space. The algorithm introduced in the last section for building such history lists (Algorithm 6) seems to be inappropriate, since it aims at finding identifying history lists for single states. However, as already discussed, in the case of continuous state spaces, only few identifying history lists for single states exist. We therefore decided to adopt the Algorithm 8 for learning history spaces, which is a part of the QU-list algorithm. In [McC95], empirical evidence is provided showing that this algorithm is especially suited for multi-dimensional, continuous state spaces.

The Identify&Exploit Algorithm on Abstract States

Before analyzing two typical continuous reinforcement learning benchmarks, we summarize the modifications necessary for adapting the Identify&Exploit algorithm to abstract state spaces.

- Algorithm 6, used for learning complete history spaces, is replaced by Algorithm 8. Since Algorithm 8 builds history lists based on Q-values, it is necessary to interleave the refinements of the history space with the process of learning Q-values. The Safe Q-Learning algorithm is therefore modified such that it contains ocassional calls of Algorithm 8, similar to the QU-List algorithm.

- We implemented two modified versions of the Safe Q-Learning algorithm, one using criterion $CE(\delta)$ for detecting identifying history lists (Algorithm 10) and another one using the MaxProb heuristic (Algorithm 11).

- The efficient identification strategy (Algorithm 5) and the basic Identify&Exploit algorithm (Algorithm 3) remain the same.

The adaptation of the Safe Q-Learning algorithm applicable to abstract state spaces is given by Algorithm 10. The main difference between Algorithm 10 and the original Safe Q-Learning algorithm (Algorithm 4) is that the history space and the Q-function are learned simultaneously. Moreover, since Q-learning is not guaranteed to converge if criterion $CE(\delta)$ is used for detecting identifying history lists, updates of the Q-function are done incrementally, i.e. by using a learning rate $\alpha < 1$. A small learning rate increases the likelihood that Q-learning converges even if there are no theoretical guarantees. The computation of the sets A_h^{vl} is adopted from the original version of the Safe Q-Learning algorithm except that the term $\max_{a \in A_h^{vl}} Q(h, a)$ is defined to be zero if $A_h^{vl} = \emptyset$. This modification turned out to stabilize the process of learning Q-values.

The MaxProb Heuristic

The set of valid transitions $\mathcal{F}^{vl}$ built according to the MaxProb heuristic contains only a single transition instance for each list-action pair. By ignoring all other transitions, all conflicts between transition instances are resolved. In

Algorithm 10 Q-Learning with Criterion CE(δ)
1: $\mathcal{F} \leftarrow \emptyset$
2: $H \leftarrow \{[ao] \mid a \in A, o \in O\}$
3: $\forall a \in A, \forall h \in H : \hat{Q}(h, a) \leftarrow 0$
4: **repeat**
5:     Sample a set of transition instances $\mathcal{F}_{new}$ by a modified ϵ-greedy exploration strategy. The greedy action of a non-identifying history list is determined by the efficient identification strategy
6:     $\mathcal{F} \leftarrow \mathcal{F} \cup \mathcal{F}_{new}$
7:     $\forall h \in H$: Recompute the sets of valid actions A_h^{vl}
8:     $\mathcal{F}^{vl} \leftarrow \{(h_t, a_t, r_t, h_{t+1}) \in \mathcal{F} \mid a_t \in A_{h_t}^{vl}$ and h_{t+1} is identifying according to criterion CE(δ)$\}$
9:     **for** $i = 0$ to N_{max} **do**
10:       **for all** $(h_t, a_t, r_t, h_{t+1}) \in \mathcal{F}$ **do**
11:         $\hat{Q}(h_t, a_t) \leftarrow (1-\alpha)\hat{Q}(h_t, a_t) + \alpha(r_t + \beta \max_{a \in A_{h_{t+1}}^{vl}} \hat{Q}(h_{t+1}, a))$
12:       **end for**
13:     **end for**
14:     After every n_{ref} sampled transition instances, call Algorithm 8 to refine the history space H
15: **until** the size of $\mathcal{F}$ exceeds a certain threshold

other words, criterion CE classifies every history list as identifying with respect to the set $\mathcal{F}^{vl}$. Thus, every history list can be treated like an identifying history list allowing the computation of Q-values for the whole history space H. Since no history lists are classified as non-identifying, the efficient identification strategy becomes unnecessary. The Identify&Exploit algorithm consists solely of selecting greedy actions with respect to the learned Q-function. Thus, using the MaxProb heuristic makes the learning process similar to the QU-List algorithm. However, Lemma 10 shows some convergence properties holding for the MaxProb heuristic.

Lemma 10. *Convergence of Q-Learning with the MaxProb Heuristic*
Let $M := (T, S, A, O, f_S, f_O, r)$ be a deterministic partially observable Markov Decision Process. Let $0 \leq \beta < 1$ be a discounting rate and let $H \subset H^*$ be a history space. If the set of valid transition instances $\mathcal{F}^{vl}$ is sampled according to the MaxProb heuristic (Algorithm 11), then every single run of the Q-learning update loop will converge to a unique fixed point.

A proof of Lemma 10 can be found in the appendix. Note that convergence is restricted only to single runs of the update loop (inner loop of Algorithm 11). The performance of the policies learned may change drastically between consecutive iterations of the outer sampling loop.

Algorithm 11 Q-Learning with MaxProb
1: $\mathcal{F} \leftarrow \emptyset$
2: $H \leftarrow \{[ao] \mid a \in A, o \in O\}$
3: $\forall a \in A, \forall h \in H : \hat{Q}(h, a) \leftarrow 0$
4: **repeat**
5:     Sample a set of episodes consisting of transition instances $\mathcal{F}_{new}$ by an ϵ-greedy exploration strategy. The greedy actions are extracted from the approximated Q-function $\hat{Q}$. Every history list is assumed to identify a state
6:     $\mathcal{F} \leftarrow \mathcal{F} \cup \mathcal{F}_{new}$
7:     $\mathcal{F}^{vl} \leftarrow \bigcup_{(h,a)\in(H\times A)}$
$$\{(h,a,r',h') \in \mathcal{F} \mid \frac{|\{(h_t,a_t,r_t,h_{t+1})\in\mathcal{F} \mid h_t=h, a_t=a, r_t=r', h_{t+1}=h'\}|}{|\{(h_t,a_t,r_t,h_{t+1})\in\mathcal{F} \mid h_t=h, a_t=a\}|}$$
is maximal with respect to $\mathcal{F}\}$
8:     $\forall h \in H : A_h^{vl} \leftarrow \{a \in A \mid \exists h' \in H, \exists r' \in \mathbb{R} \ (h,a,r',h') \in \mathcal{F}^{vl}\}$
9:     **repeat**
10:         **for all** $(h_t, a_t, r_t, h_{t+1}) \in \mathcal{F}^{vl}$ **do**
11:             $\hat{Q}(h_t, a_t) \leftarrow r_t + \beta \max_{a \in A_{h_{t+1}}^{vl}} \hat{Q}(h_{t+1}, a)$
12:         **end for**
13:     **until** $\hat{Q}$ converges
14:     After every n_{ref} sampled transition instances, call Algorithm 8 to refine the history space H.
15: **until** the size of $\mathcal{F}$ exceeds a certain threshold

The MaxProb heuristic ignores some aspects of the learning problem by throwing away transition instances. This may sound unusual, but it offers the following benefits:

- If Q-learning converges to a fixed-point, it is possible to extract a greedy policy with respect to the final Q-function. Obviously, this is not the case if the Q-function diverges.

- By ignoring some of the transition instances, we learn a policy consistent with a subset of the complete set of transition instances. We know that the policy learned by this procedure will be successful in at least some situations, since it has been built from transitions that have actually occurred. We therefore can hope that the policy generalizes well to many unseen situations. Moreover, we think that it may be possible to analyze the policy learned also from a theoretical point of view. As shown in the proof of Theorem 7, we can extract a history list MDP from the subset of transition instances used for updating the Q-function. It would be very interesting to compare this history list MDP to the original MDP. Although this is an important issue, we will not further investigate this question, but leave it for future work.

Temporal Abstraction

We found out from preliminary experiments that even a drastic reduction of a continuous state space by extracting features does not simplify the learning problem if the total number of action choices remains the same. This is particularly true for history lists, because every action choice corresponds to an entry in a history list. Thus, too many action choices significantly lengthen the history lists. Thus, both the Identify&Exploit algorithm as well as the QU-List algorithm need to make use of temporal abstraction, as already discussed, in order to learn successful policies. All empirical results presented in the next subsections are achieved by sampling abstract transitions instead of ordinary transitions. A discussion about abstract transitions can be found in subsection 4.2.5.

4.3.3 Empirical Results for the Mountain Car

The mountain car benchmark consists of driving a car to the top of a mountain by accelerating in the forward and backward direction. The original setup of the mountain car benchmark can be found in [SS96]. However, we used a revised formulation of the system dynamics developed in [Moo95] and [SR03], since the original dynamics stated in [SS96] contain some technical flaws.

The state space is two-dimensional and consists of the position x of the car and the velocity $\dot{x}$ of the car. The track is bounded by the interval $x \in [-1.0, 1.2]$ and the velocity is bounded by the interval $\dot{x} \in [-5, 5]$. The bottom of the hill is defined to be at $x_{bottom} = -0.5$ and the goal is to reach the top of the mountain at $x_{top} \geq 1.0$. The car is always started from the bottom of the hill. Possible actions are forces taken from the set $a \in \{-4, 4\}$. The control frequency is set to 20Hz and every episode has a maximum length of 300 control cycles. An episode is aborted if the system reaches a goal state or the car exceeds the track boundaries. A constant reward of (-1) is given unless the car leaves the track (-100) or a goal state is reached $(+100)$.

The observation space is given by a very coarse, regular discretization of the state space. Both the resolution of the position of the car as well as the resolution of the velocity were set to five. To make the process of building history spaces from these coarse observations more efficient, Algorithm 8, refining the history space is called three times in a row instead of making a single call.

As a baseline, we computed an approximately optimal policy by a $150 * 150$ grid using ordinary Q-learning. The optimal policy takes approximately 35 steps to the goal, corresponding to a cumulative reward of 65.

Our experimental setup consists of fifty runs of each of the following algorithms:

1. The QU-List algorithm.

2. The Identify&Exploit algorithm using criterion $CE(\delta)$ to detect identifying history lists. Results are presented for $\delta \in \{0.3, 0.4, 0.5\}$, since we found out from preliminary experiments that low values for δ give best results.

3. The Identify&Exploit algorithm using the MaxProb heuristic.

The only parameter that is varied among the algorithms is the maximal search depth L of the efficient identification strategy. We selected the search depth L yielding the best results for a particular setting of the parameter δ. Learning curves of the experiments are plotted in Figure 4.18. All values are averaged over fifty runs. The final performance of the policies learned is summarized in Table 4.14.

Algorithm	Size ($|H|$)	Search Depth (L)	Cumulative Reward
Optimal	-	-	65
QU-List	107.7 (29.7)	-	36.4 (54.5)
MaxProb	128.7 (60.8)	-	64 (0.0)
Criterion CE(0.3)	124.4 (43.8)	1	61.5 (8.4)
Criterion CE(0.4)	166.8 (72.7)	3	52.58 (73.9)
Criterion CE(0.5)	183.4 (68)	5	12.77 (148.3)

Table 4.14: Final performance of policies learned for the mountain car. The second column shows the size of the history space learned. The third column shows the setting of parameter L and the fourth column shows the averaged cumulative reward achieved. The first row shows the performance of an optimal policy. The numbers in braces give the standard deviation.

As can be seen in Table 4.14, the MaxProb heuristic achieved the highest cumulative reward followed by criterion $CE(\delta)$ with $\delta = 0.3$. We think there

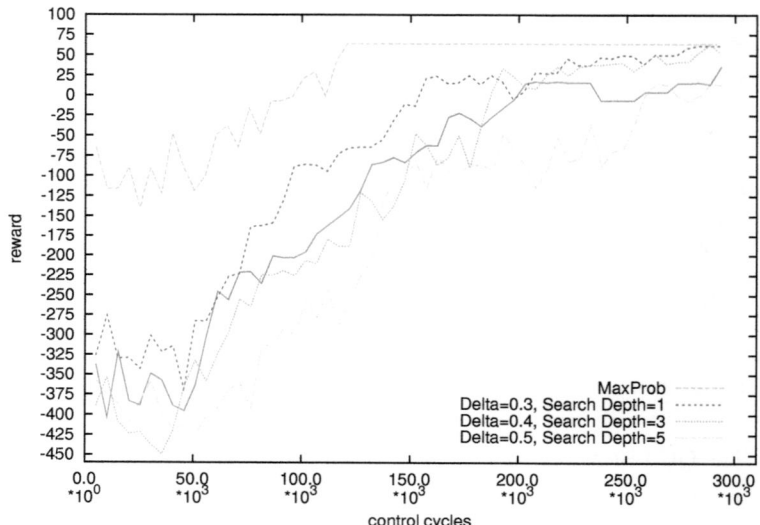

Figure 4.18: Learning policies for the mountain car. The x-axis shows the number of control cycles, while the y-axis shows the cumulative reward achieved. Setting of parameters: Learning rate $\alpha = 0.1$, constant exploration rate $\epsilon = 0.05$, discounting rate $\beta = 0.98$. After every ten sampled episodes, the Q-learning update loop is executed with $N_{max} = 200$. After every $n_{ref} = 10000$ sampled transition instances, the history space is refined by Algorithm 8. A total number of $3 * 10^5$ transition instances is sampled in order to learn a policy.

are two main reasons explaining these results. First, every single run of the Q-learning update loop is guaranteed to converge if the MaxProb heuristic is used to build the set of valid transitions $\mathcal{F}^{vl}$ (Lemma 10). The learning curve for the MaxProb heuristic is therefore much more stable compared to the other curves. The second reason is that for the mountain car benchmark, very good policies can be learned on small history spaces containing less than one hundred history lists. Thus, many transition instances are available for a single history list from H and the transition probabilities can be estimated with high precision. The transition instances selected by the MaxProb heuristic therefore constitute good representatives of the process.

The QU-List algorithm computes Q-values for all history lists, but the Q-learning updates are not guaranteed to converge. Some runs of QU-List algorithm therefore diverged to useless[4] policies, causing a high standard deviation of the final performance.

If criterion $CE(\delta)$ is used for detecting identifying history lists, the Iden-

---

[4] We consider a policy to be useless if it does not reach the goal state.

tify&Exploit learns much slower than with the MaxProb heuristic. This is due to the fact that some lists are classified as non-identifying by criterion CE(δ). For these lists, no Q-values are computed and the efficient identification strategy is used to derive a policy. Although the efficient identification strategy helps to avoid diverging to completely useless policies, the performance of the overall policies found is often of low quality. The reason for this undesired behavior is that the efficient identification aims at maximizing the probability of finding an identifying history list, but does not care about reward signals. In fact, some runs of the Identify&Exploit algorithm converged to policies reaching the goal state after a large number of steps. This effect becomes stronger for high values of δ, since for high values of δ, more history lists are classified as non-identifying and the efficient identification strategy is called very often. For $\delta = 0.5$, the Identify&Exploit algorithm sometimes fails to learn a useful policy at all.

It turned out that the optimal search depth of the efficient identification strategy strongly depends on the parameter δ. For high values of δ, the search for identifying history lists has to be much deeper in order to learn successful policies. Conversely, for low values of δ, a relatively flat search suffices to learn good policies. This fact is illustrated by the Figures 4.19 and 4.20.

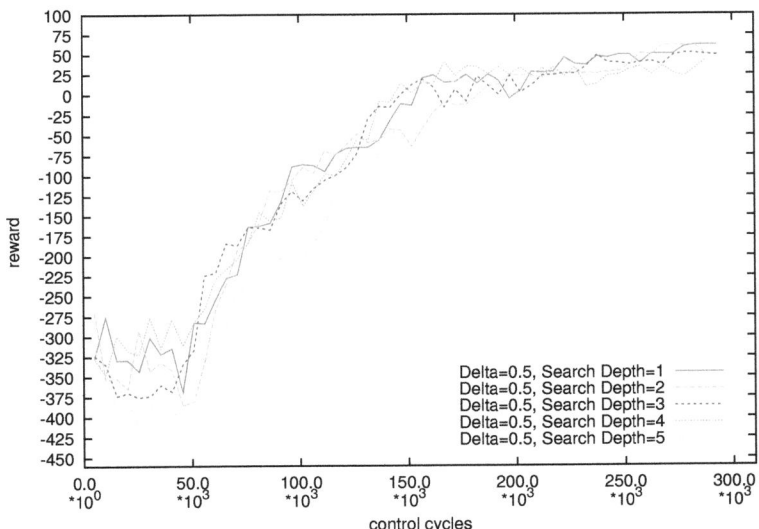

Figure 4.19: Learning policies for the mountain car using criterion CE(0.3) to detect identifying history lists. The x-axis shows the number of control cycles, while the y-axis shows the cumulative reward achieved. The five learning curves correspond to different settings of the parameter L, the maximal search depth of the efficient identification strategy.

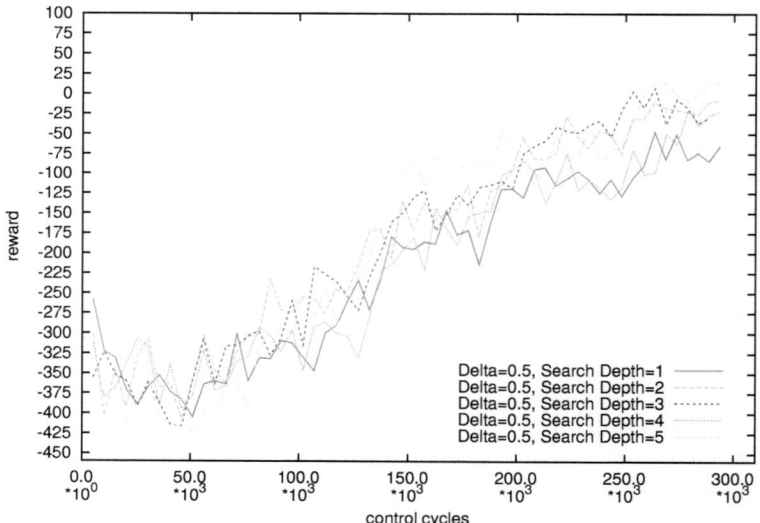

Figure 4.20: Learning policies for the mountain car using criterion CE(0.5) to detect identifying history lists. The x-axis shows the number of control cycles, while the y-axis shows the cumulative reward achieved. The five learning curves correspond to different settings of the parameter L, i.e. the maximal search depth of the efficient identification strategy.

A reasonable explanation for this result is that for high values of δ, only few history lists are classified as identifying by criterion CE(δ). Thus, a deep search is necessary in order to find an identifying history list.

4.3.4 Empirical Results for the Cart-Pole

We also considered the pole balancing benchmark for which the system dynamics are given in [BSA83]. The state space is four-dimensional and consists of the angle θ of the pole, the angular velocity $\dot{\theta}$ of the pole, the position x of the cart and the velocity $\dot{x}$ of the cart. The initial angle of the pole is randomly chosen from the interval $\theta \in [-0.05\ 0.05]$, while the initial velocities $\dot{\theta}$ and $\dot{x}$ are set to zero. The cart always starts from the middle of the track, which is bounded by the interval $x \in [-2.4\ 2.4]$. Possible actions are forces taken from the set $a \in \{-10, 10\}$. The control frequency is set to 50Hz.

The learning task is to prevent the pole from falling down and the cart from leaving the track. If such an undesired event occurs, the current episode is terminated and a new one is started. Episodes sampled for learning a policy have a maximal length of 300 control cycles, while episodes sampled for testing a policy are of length 2000. Moreover, learning episodes are started from a bigger set of initial angles $\theta \in [-0.1\ 0.1]$, since it turned out that this procedure helps to generalize over rarely visited parts of the state space. After every balancing step (control cycle), a reward of (-1) is given unless the episode crashes (-100) or the current state is within a certain goal area $(+10)$. The goal area is defined by the following two constraints: $|\theta| \leq 0.05$ and $|x| \leq 0.4$.

As for the mountain car benchmark, the observation space is given by the cells of a regular grid laid over the continuous state space. Every dimension of the state space is discretized by a constant resolution of five. In order to cover only the most important parts of the state space, we restrict the discretization to the following subset of the state space: $\theta \in [-0.1\ 0.1]$, $\dot{\theta} \in [-1.0\ 1.0]$, $x \in [-0.2\ 0.2]$, $\dot{x} \in [-0.5\ 0.5]$.

The experimental set-up is the same as for the mountain car benchmark, i.e. we tested both the QU-List algorithm, the Identify&Exploit algorithm using criterion $CE(\delta)$ for detecting identifying history lists and the MaxProb heuristic. We performed a coarse search for optimal settings of the parameter δ and the search depth L of the efficient identification strategy. We present results for the set $\delta \in \{0.2, 0.3, 0.4\}$ combined with the corresponding optimal search depths.

While Figure 4.21 shows a learning curve plotting the cumulative reward achieved by the policies learned, Figure 4.22 illustrates the number of steps the policies are capable of balancing the pole. All values shown are averaged over twenty runs of each algorithm. Table 4.15 presents a summary of the final performance of the policies.

Since the history spaces H necessary for learning good balancing policies are much bigger compared to the mountain car benchmark, less transition instances are available for a single history list from H. Thus, the estimated transition model on history lists is less accurate and the MaxProb heuristic fails to select the transition instances being good representatives of the process. The performance of the MaxProb heuristic is therefore worse than for the other algorithms.

For $\delta = 0.3$, the Identify&Exploit algorithm using criterion $CE(\delta)$ is able to balance the pole more reliably than the QU-List algorithm. While both

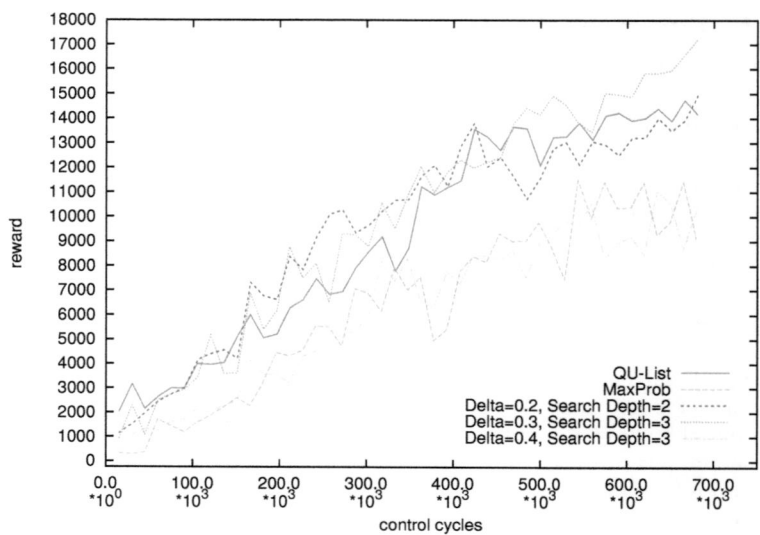

Figure 4.21: Learning balancing policies for the cart-pole. The x-axis shows the number of control cycles, while the y-axis shows the cumulative reward achieved. Setting of parameters: Learning rate $\alpha = 0.1$, constant exploration rate $\epsilon = 0.1$, discounting rate $\beta = 0.98$. After every ten sampled episodes, the Q-learning update loop is executed with $N_{max} = 200$. After every $n_{ref} = 50000$ sampled transition instances, the history space is refined by Algorithm 8. A total number of $7 * 10^5$ transition instances is sampled in order to learn a policy.

Algorithm	Size ($|H|$)	Balancing Steps	Cumulative Reward
QU-List	19580.6 (671.3)	1932.2 (138.2)	14172.16 (7117.2)
MaxProb	18581.8 (675.7)	1451.8 (411.9)	9120.8 (5925.2)
Criterion CE(0.2)	19633.1 (758.4)	1962.8 (77.4)	14935 (3806.9)
Criterion CE(0.3)	19385.5 (811)	1912 (118.1)	17209.5 (3370.2)
Criterion CE(0.4)	18610.4 (525.9)	1262.53 (538.7)	10270 (5641.6)

Table 4.15: Final performance of policies learned for the cart-pole. The second column shows the size of the history spaces learned. The third column shows the number of steps the final policy is capable of balancing the pole and the fourth column shows the cumulative reward achieved by the final policy. The numbers in braces give the standard deviation.

algorithms are able to balance the pole for the same number of control cycles, the Identify&Exploit algorithm is also capable of keeping the system inside the goal

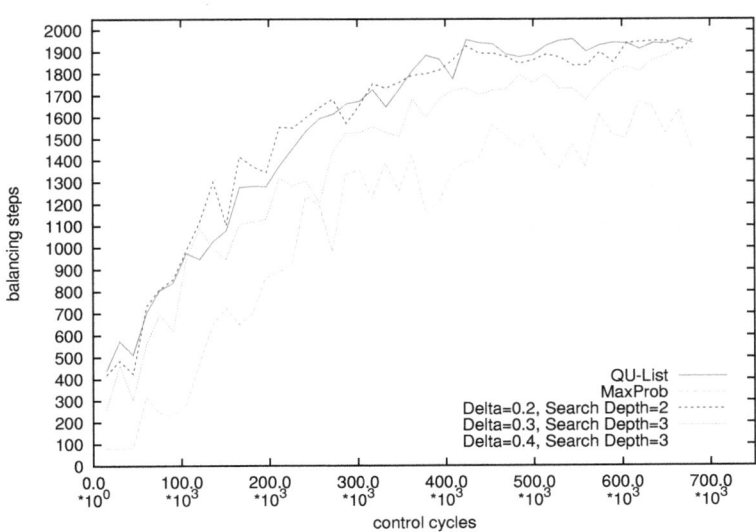

Figure 4.22: Learning balancing policies for the cart-pole. The x-axis shows the number of control cycles, while the y-axis shows the number of steps the policy is capable of balancing the pole.

area. This corresponds to keeping the cart in the middle of the track. Remember that the reward for balancing the pole inside the goal area is (+10), while the reward for balancing the pole outside the goal area is only (-1). We think that this result is caused by the efficient identification strategy: The QU-List performs Q-learning updates for all history lists in H, although many of these history lists identify a very large set of states. The problem with history lists identifying a large set of states is that Q-learning is not able to learn successful policies for these lists. For example, consider a history list $h \in H$ identifying a large subset $S' \subset S$. It is hardly possible to find a good action for h, since S' contains many states having different optimal actions. The Q-values learned are less significant because they constitute average values built over a large set of states. Thus, the greedy action chosen by the QU-List algorithm is likely to be suboptimal. In contrast to the QU-List algorithm, the Identify&Exploit algorithm executes an efficient identification strategy if history list h becomes the current history list. This is due to the fact that criterion $CE(\delta)$ is designed to classify h as non-identifying if the set of states identified by h is very large. The identification strategy then searches for another history list $h' \in H$ identifying a smaller set of states than h does. The Q-values for h' are much more reliable allowing us to extract a useful greedy action for h'.

If the parameter δ takes on high values, criterion $CE(\delta)$ identifies only those lists as identifying which identify a very small set of states. In such a setting, most lists are classified as non-identifying, which is why Q-values are available only for a small fraction of the history space. We think that this is the reason why the results are best for relatively low values of δ. For high values of δ, there are simply not enough Q-values available to learn very good policies.

As can be seen from Table 4.15, the standard deviation for the cumulative rewards achieved is very high compared to the experiments for the partially observable mazes. This is due to the fact that none of the tested algorithms is guaranteed to converge to a unique policy. While most policies learned are capable of balancing the pole, all policies sometimes failed to keep the cart-pole within the goal region. The standard deviation is high, since no algorithm we tested was able to achieve a high cumulative in every single run.

Chapter 5

Future Work on the Identify&Exploit Algorithm

This chapter discusses possible extensions of the Identify&Exploit algorithm, which can be implemented both by tuning the performance as well as by generalizations of the history list concept. We will especially discuss some ideas for overcoming the limitations of the history list framework. The thesis concludes with a summary of the results presented.

5.1 Solving general POMDPs with History Lists

5.1.1 Generalizations of the History List Concept

What are the limitations of the history list concept and how can the history list concept be generalized? There are two main problems that inevitably arise when working with history lists.

1. History lists are implementing short-term memory. In particular, history lists do not allow to learn optimal policies, since the length of a history list is limited. Much information about past events is therefore ignored.

2. It is hardly possible to explicitly model probabilities with history lists. Thus, the algorithms presented in this thesis work best for deterministic systems. In a stochastic domain, the use of history lists is mostly heuristical.

To solve the problem of limited memory, the work in [HJ06] introduces history lists with loops. The history lists are contained within a suffix-tree making predictions about future observations. A path through this tree starts at the root node and corresponds to a certain, possibly cyclic sequence of past observations and actions. The leave nodes of the tree contain predictions about future observations. By allowing the tree to have loops, it is possible to deal with long subsequences of useless information which can be sandwiched into an enclosing sequence. Looping suffix-trees can substantially reduce the number of history lists, i.e. branches of a tree. Moreover, the loops make it possible to remember events that happened an infinite number of time steps ago. However, the trees presented in [HJ06] are designed for prediction purposes. Neither is an efficient identification used to safely identify the current state, nor is a policy learned.

The Identify&Exploit algorithm does not consider loops, because loop detection is a potential source of error. An incorrectly detected loop (by inspecting sampled episodes) could damage the performance of the efficient identification strategy and the quality of the Q-values learned. However, it would be easily possible to include the looping mechanism by inserting links from longer history lists to shorter history lists. A potential benefit of k-complete history spaces compared to looping suffix-trees is that it is possible to bound the size of the history space by the parameter k. Even for small values of k, it will be possible to learn good policies on a k-complete space because of the efficient identification strategy. While applying a policy, the efficient identification strategy establishes exactly those identifying history lists for which stored Q-values are available. We conclude that it is still an interesting idea to extend the Identify&Exploit algorithm by including history lists with loops. By such a procedure, we can hope to solve problems which require unlimited memory.

In order to generalize history lists to stochastic domains, the notion of tests proved to be very useful. The test concept was initially introduced in [RS94] for learning the model of a deterministic POMDP. A test itself consists of a sequence of actions, while the outcome of a test is defined as the observation made after executing the action sequence. In [LSS02], this idea is generalized to the stochastic case yielding predictive state representations (PSRs). In the context of PSRs, tests are considered to be sequences of observations and actions such that probabilities can be assigned to these sequences. The expression $p(t|h) = p(o_1,..,o_k|ha_1,...,a_k)$ for a test $t = a_1 o_1...a_k o_k$ denotes the probability of observing a certain sequence of observations, given that a certain sequence of actions is executed and a certain history h (past events) occurred. Similar to the work in [RS94], it can be shown that the model of a general POMDP can be expressed by a sufficiently large set of tests $\{t_1, ..., t_n\}$. This set is then called a PSR. The prediction vector $p(h) = [p(t_1|h), ..., p(t_n|h)]$ constitutes a sufficient statistic of the system. Unfortunately, until now, existing literature about PSRs focuses mainly on predicting the state, but not on learning policies. It is questionable if traditional reinforcement learning algorithms like Q-learning can be used in combination with PSRs. The development of a framework which enables learning policies for PSRs would be a big step towards efficient, model-free algorithms for stochastic POMDPs.

5.1.2 Noisy POMDPs

The Identify&Exploit using criterion CE for detecting identifying history lists converges to a unique policy even for stochastic POMDPs. This is guaranteed by Theorem 6, since the proof of Theorem 6 does not exploit the fact that the problems we considered are deterministic. However, if the transition model is stochastic, it is unlikely that a sequence of observations of actions is capable of uniquely identifying a single state. In such a setting, the learned history spaces probably contain only a very few number of identifying history lists.

We think that for a certain subclass of stochastic POMDPs, it may be possible to extend the analysis presented and therefore make the Identify&Exploit algorithm applicable to stochastic problem settings. The idea is to consider only those POMDPs, in which a deterministic model is disturbed by some noise.

Definition 27. *Noisy POMDP*
Let $M := (T, S, A, O, P_S, f_O, r)$ be a partially observable Markov decision process. The POMDP M is called noisy with respect to noise terms $0.5 < z_S \leq 1$ and $0.5 < z_O \leq 1$, if the model of M satisfies the following two conditions:

$$\forall s \in S, \forall a \in A, \exists s' \in S : P_S(s' \mid s, a) \geq z_S \tag{5.1}$$

$$\forall s \in S, \forall a \in A, \exists o \in O : P_O(o \mid s, a) \geq z_O \tag{5.2}$$

As mentioned above, it is hard to explicitly model stochasticity with history lists. A first step towards solving this problem could be to extract a deterministic model from a noisy POMDP and then learn a policy for the resulting deterministic POMDP.

Definition 28. *Deterministic POMDP Extracted from a Noisy POMDP*
Let $M := (T, S, A, O, P_S, f_O, r)$ be a noisy partially observable Markov decision with respect to noise terms z_S and z_O. The extracted deterministic partially observable Markov decision process M_D from M is defined as follows: Every component of M_D equals the corresponding component of M except the transition model and the observation model. The transition model of M_D is deterministic and can therefore be represented by a transition function $f_S : S \times A \rightarrow S$. The transition function is defined as $f_S(s, a) := s'$, if $P_S(s' \mid s, a) \geq z_S$. The observation model is also deterministic and can therefore be expressed by an observation function $f_O : A \times S \rightarrow O$. The observation function is defined as $f_O(a, s) := o$, if $P_O(o \mid s, a) \geq z_O$. Since $z_S > 0.5$ and $z_O > 0.5$, the model of M_D is well-defined.

Our goal is to adapt criterion CE to a noisy POMDP and to the extracted deterministic POMDP, respectively. We have to generalize the definition of criterion CE such that the criterion is able to detect identifying history lists of the extracted deterministic POMDP, while still sampling transitions from the original, noisy POMDP. The difficulty in detecting these identifying history lists is that there are two different sources for conflicting transitions. For example, consider two conflicting transition instances $\mathcal{T} := (h, a, r', h')$ and $\mathcal{T}' := (h, a, h'', r'')$ with respect to a history list $h \in H$. Assume that the conflict is given by $h' \neq h''$.

History list h is non-identifying Assume that $h \in H$ is not identifying a single state with respect to the extracted deterministic POMDP. Then there exist at least two possible current states, if h becomes the current history list ($h_t = h$). Thus, after executing an action $a_t \in A$, the observation made is possibly ambiguous causing a conflict between the transitions T and T'.

History list h is identifying Since the transitions are sampled from a noisy transition model P_S and a noisy observation model P_O, the transitions T and T' may cause a conflict even if h identifies a state with respect to the extracted deterministic POMDP.

Thus, a conflict can be generated both by an identifying history list as well as by a non-identifying history list. This makes it impossible for criterion CE to correctly classify a list.

We will now develop an alternative criterion for detecting identifying history lists trying to separate the two different sources of conflicts.

Lemma 11. *History Lists for Noisy POMDPs*
Let $M := (T, S, A, O, P_S, f_O, r)$ be a noisy partially observable Markov decision with respect to noise terms z_S and z_O. Let M_D be the corresponding extracted, deterministic POMDP. Let f_S be the deterministic transition function of M_D. Consider a sequence of state transitions $s_0, ..., s_{L-1}, s_L$ generated by the function f_S given a fixed action sequence $a_0, ..., a_{L-1}$ of length L. The probability of the same state sequence to be generated by the noisy model P_S is at least z_S^L. It holds that $p(s_0, ..., s_{L-1}, s_L \mid s_0, a_0, ..., a_{L-1}) \geq z_S^L$, if $f_S(s_t, a_t) = s_{t+1}$ for $0 \leq t \leq L - 1$.

Proof.

$$p(s_0, ..., s_{L-1}, s_L \mid s_0, a_0, ..., a_{L-1}) = \prod_{t=0}^{L-1} P_S(s_{t+1} \mid s_t, a_t)$$
$$\geq z_S^L \qquad (5.3)$$

The stated inequality follows directly from the definition of the function f_S which is part of the extracted deterministic POMDP.

$\square$

With this simple result, it is straightforward to adapt criterion CE to noisy POMDPs. Every state sequence of length L (given a fixed action sequence) generated by f_S is also generated by the original model P_S with at least probability z_S^L. We can apply this result for detecting identifying history lists in the following way: Assume a history list $h \in H$ is identifying a single state $s \in S$ of an extracted deterministic POMDP. We know from Lemma 11 that every time the list h becomes the current history list, the state s becomes the current state with at least probability $z_S^{|h|}$. This is due to the fact that the identifying history list h corresponds to a state sequence ending in state s, which is generated by the transition function f_S. Thus, for every action $a \in A$ executed in h, there exists a history list $h' \in H$ such that h' is the successor list of h with a probability equal or higher than $z_S^{|h|+1}$. We conclude that if a history list is identifying a state of the extracted deterministic POMDP, then the number of conflicting transitions with respect to this history list is bounded.

Definition 29. *Criterion for Detecting Identifying History Lists for Deterministic, Extracted POMDPs (CN)*
Let $M := (T, S, A, O, P_S, f_O, r)$ be a noisy partially observable Markov decision process with respect to noise terms $0.5 < z_S \leq 1$ and $z_O = 1$. Let M_D be the deterministic, extracted POMDP from M and let $H \subset H^*$ be a history space with respect to M. A history list $h \in H$ is called identifying according to criterion CN and a set of transition instances $\mathcal{F}$ sampled from the noisy transition model P_S, if the following condition is satisfied:

$$\forall a \in A, \exists h' \in H, \exists r' \in \mathbb{R}: \frac{|\{(h_t,a_t,r_t,h_{t+1}) \in \mathcal{F} \mid h_t=h, a_t=a, r_t=r', h_{t+1}=h'\}|}{|\{(h_t,a_t,r_t,h_{t+1}) \in \mathcal{F} \mid h_t=h, a_t=a\}|} \geq z^{|h|+1}$$

Note that for very long history lists ($|h| \to \infty$) it holds that $z_S^{|h|} \to 0$. Thus, criterion CN is supposed to work best for short history lists and high values of z_S. Since we have no empirical evaluation of criterion CN so far, its presentation is merely an inspiration for future work on history lists.

Another idea for generalizing the history list concept is to introduce confidence parameters for history lists. A confidence parameter $0 \leq \delta \leq 1$ represents the probability that a history list $h \in H$ identifies a state. Stated precisely, the parameter δ gives the probability that the process is in a certain state when h becomes the current history list. We think that for deterministic POMDPs disturbed by some random noise, it is possible to bound the confidence parameters of a given set of history lists. Although Q-Learning would not converge on a history space consisting of only gradually identifying history lists, it would still be possible to perform value iteration on a learned, but fixed probabilistic model defined on history lists.

Although the history list concept may be too simple to perfectly model general POMDPs, we think that it is a promising approach to search for interesting subclasses of POMDPs, for example, noisy POMDPs.

5.2 Performance Tuning

5.2.1 Data Efficiency

All algorithms previously presented are not tuned with respect to the sampling complexity, although the sampling process is fundamental to every model-free, reinforcement learning algorithm. Here, we want to present some straightforward ideas for increasing the performance of the Identify&Exploit algorithm by decreasing the number of sampled episodes.

First, it is possible to reuse sampled episodes. In order to learn complete history spaces, Algorithm 6 discards all episodes sampled at the beginning of the main loop, even if these episodes contain very useful information. Such a procedure prevents our algorithms from running out of memory, but is obviously suboptimal. The total number of sampled episodes could be reduced by employing simple heuristics.

- It is possible to implement a data counter for every history list indicating how many transition instances are available for a list. Only those transition instances are discarded, which belong to a history list having a sufficiently high data counter.

- Since the number of possible history lists (in H^*) exponentially grows with the length of the lists, it is reasonable to sample only a few episodes during the first iterations of the main loop, while sampling many more episodes during the later iterations.

- The number of stored transition instances can be kept constant at a maximum level by simultaneously adding and discarding transition instances. Thus, an abrupt decrease in the total number of sampled transition instances can be avoided.

5.2.2 Extending the Efficient Identification Strategy

The efficient identification strategy implemented by Algorithm 5 is an integral part of the Identify&Exploit algorithm. We implemented a rather simple strategy trying to find the safest path to an identifying history list. Here, "safe" means to maximize the probability of eventually arriving at an identifying history list. As a second minor optimization criterion we used the length of the identification sequence.

The performance achieved for the big maze (Figure 4.4) using this strategy is very good as shown by the empirical results. However, for other problem settings it may be necessary to strictly avoid some regions of the state space, since these regions cause very large negative reward signals. The efficient identification can be generalized such that the reward is included as a further optimization criterion. A promising idea is to weight the cumulative reward of an identification sequence with the probability of reaching an identifying history list. As discussed in the fourth chapter, it is also possible to use the value iteration procedure for approximating a reward-optimal path to an identifying history list.

5.2.3 Combining Criterion CC and Criterion CE

Given a POMDP with a finite number of states, the performance of the Identify&Exploit algorithm can be increased by combining criterion CC with criterion CE. To illustrate this, we will again discuss the benefits and drawbacks of each criterion.

If a k-complete history space is available, it is preferable to choose criterion CC, because it has been proven to work correctly and can be checked efficiently.

Note that if the history space used is not k-complete, but at least it holds that the conditions (4.1) and (4.2) are satisfied, then Q-learning will still converge and criterion CC will detect only a subset of all identifying history lists. It follows from Theorem 4 that criterion CC can reliably detect an identifying history list $h \in H$ only if $|h| \leq k - l_{su}$. Thus, if criterion CC is not applicable, criterion CE can be employed. Criterion CE gives only empirical evidence that a history list is identifying, but at least guarantees convergence of the Q-learning algorithm. The problem with criterion CE is that even if Q-learning converges, the extracted policy is not necessarily successful. This is due to the fact that a history list classified as identifying by criterion CE can actually be non-identifying. In such a situation, Q-values are learned also for non-identifying history lists and the efficient identification strategy might fail to establish an identifying history list.

Given a k-complete history space, we propose to classify a history list $h \in H$ by criterion CC if $|h| \leq k - l_{su}$ and by criterion CE otherwise. By using this procedure, we achieve guaranteed convergence and it is likely that most existing identifying history lists will be detected.

5.2.4 Extracting Features from States

For our empirical analysis of continuous MDPs, we used very coarse discretizations of the state space. We chose to discretize states, because the resulting history space does not incorporate any form of prior knowledge. However, for some problem settings, it may not be possible to identify sufficiently small sets of single states by a discretization procedure. A cell index is a very simple feature of a state.

A set of more carefully selected features is likely to help identifying the important parts of the state space. A promising idea for increasing the performance of the Identify&Exploit algorithm is therefore to combine it with a powerful method for extracting features from states.

5.3 Summary

In this thesis, we developed a model-free reinforcement learning algorithm for solving both POMDPs as well as MDPs. We first presented the Identify&Exploit algorithm for solving deterministic POMDPs, which was then generalized to continuous MDPs. The motivation for such a two-step procedure is that solving MDPs with large state spaces requires some form of abstraction over states. One particular way of establishing such abstraction is to ignore some parts of the complete state information, only considering sequences of observations of states. However, if the learning agent processes observations of state, then this is equivalent to a POMDP setting. Thus, algorithms capable of solving POMDPs are potentially useful for large MDPs.

Since policies for POMDPs are memory-based, we employed a history list framework to establish a certain form of short-term memory. Short-term memory is practical for a variety of reasons.

- The concept of a history list is simple, clear and easy to implement.
- The amount of memory allocated by a history list is determined by the size of the list.
- The simplicity of the history list concept allows us to analyze our algorithms also from a theoretical point of view. This is not the case for powerful, but complicated memory representations like, for example, recurrent neural networks.
- A history space is scalable. This means that it is possible to adapt the size of a history space to the needs of a specific problem. The same holds for the total amount of memory used.
- Since a history space is finite and discrete, it is possible to compute Q-values for history lists. Thus, standard algorithms from reinforcement learning can be adapted to learn policies defined on history spaces.

The main idea presented in this thesis is to divide a policy for a POMDP into two separate phases. At the beginning of an episode, the learning agent collects information by actively establishing a history list identifying the current state. This phase is called the efficient identification strategy. After the current state has been determined, a Q-function can be used to extract a greedy policy. Whenever the agent loses track of the current state, it switches back to the identification phase. This algorithm is called Identify&Exploit.

The difficulty in implementing the Identify&Exploit algorithm is that the learning agent is uncertain about which history lists are capable of identifying the current state. Thus, a criterion is needed which is able to detect identifying history lists. We presented two such criteria, namely criterion CC and criterion CE. For criterion CC, we proved that it works perfectly under certain assumptions imposed on the history space. We showed empirically that for reasonably large, but finite state spaces, it is possible to learn history spaces satisfying these assumptions. The performance of the policies learned on the history spaces is suboptimal, but still close to the optimum.

The use of criterion CE enables us to drop any assumptions concerning the history space for the price of losing the theoretical guarantees available for criterion CC. However, for both criteria, it is possible to show that Q-learning converges to a unique Q-function. All learning can be done model-free, i.e. without knowledge of the model of the process.

The Identify&Exploit algorithm can also be applied to continuous MDPs by generalizing criterion CE to a confidence parameter δ. While the original version of criterion CE aims at detecting history lists identifying single states, criterion $CE(\delta)$ aims at detecting history lists identifying sets of states. A history space can therefore be interpreted as an abstract state space. Each history list corresponds to an abstract state consisting of a subset of the state space. Identifying sets of states is a reasonable approach, since it is hardly possible to identify a single state from a continuous state space by a sequence of observations and actions.

The parameter δ allows us to control the size of the sets that should be identified. For high values of δ, a history list is classified as identifying by criterion $CE(\delta)$ if the list identifies a small set of states. Conversely, for small values of δ, a history list is classified as identifying by criterion $CE(\delta)$ if the list identifies a large set of states. A history list identifying a small subset of the state space is especially useful because it is likely that all states from this set have similar optimal actions. Thus, a near optimal policy can be defined for such a list.

We have empirically shown for two continuous benchmark problems that by adjusting the parameter δ, it is possible to learn very good, but not optimal policies. Unfortunately, Q-learning is not guaranteed to converge to a unique Q-function if criterion $CE(\delta)$ is used to detect identifying history lists. The learning process is therefore somewhat unstable compared to the experiments conducted for finite state spaces. However, the efficient identification strategy has been proven to be effective also for the continuous case. We conclude that identifying subsets of the state space is a practical approach for implementing state abstractions.

Appendix A

Proofs of Lemmas

Lemma 1. *Let $M := (T, S, A, P_S, r)$ be a Markov decision process such that T is a finite set of time steps including a maximal element $T_F \in T$. A countable state space S is assumed and a discounting rate $0 \leq \beta < 1$. The value functions $V_n : S \to \mathbb{R}$ $(0 \leq n < T_F)$ defined in Equation (2.1) can be equivalently expressed as follows:*

$$V_n(s) = \max_{a \in A}[r(s,a) + \beta \sum_{s' \in S} P_S(s'|s,a) V_{n+1}(s')] \quad (A.1)$$

Proof. For the following analysis it is convenient to write $S_s^{(n)} := \{s = s_n, s_{n+1}, ..., s_{T_F}\}$ for a state sequence beginning with state $s \in S$ at time $t = n$. Elements of this sequence can be accessed by an argument $n \leq i \leq T_F$ such that $S_s^{(n)}(i) := s_i$. The symbol $\sum_{S_s^{(n)}}$ expresses the sum over all possible state sequences starting in state $s \in S$ at time $t = n$. Let $\pi^{(n)} := \{\pi_t\}_{(n \leq t < T_F)}$ denote a non-stationary policy selecting actions from time $t = n$ until time $t = T_F - 1$. The term $p(S_s^{(n)} \mid \pi^{(n)})$ denotes the probability of the state sequence $S_s^{(n)}$ given that policy $\pi^{(n)}$ is executed from state $s_n = s$.

$$V_n(s) = \max_{\pi^{(n)}} E[\sum_{t=n}^{T_F-1} \beta^{t-n} r(s_t, \pi_t(s_t)) + \beta^{T_F-n} r(s_{T_F}, \cdot) \mid s_n = s]$$

$$= \max_{\pi^{(n)}}[\sum_{S_s^{(n)}} p(S_s^{(n)} \mid \pi^{(n)})[\sum_{t=n}^{T_F-1} \beta^{t-n} r(S_s^{(n)}(t), \pi_t(S_s^{(n)}(t)))$$
$$+ \beta^{T_F-n} r(S_s^{(n)}(T_F), \cdot)]]$$

$$= \max_{\pi^{(n)}}[r(s, \pi_n(s)) + \sum_{S^{(n)}(s)} p(S^{(n)}(s) | \pi^{(n)})$$
$$\cdot [\sum_{t=n+1}^{T_F-1} \beta^{t-n} r(S_s^{(n)}(t), \pi_t(S_s^{(n)}(t))) + \beta^{T_F-n} r(S_s^{(n)}(T_F), \cdot)]]$$

$$\begin{aligned}
V_n(s) &= \max_{\pi^{(n)}}[r(s,\pi_n(s)) + \sum_{S^{(n)}(s)} p(S^{(n)}(s)|\pi^{(n)}) \\
&\quad \cdot [\sum_{t=n+1}^{T_F-1} \beta^{t-n} r(S_s^{(n)}(t), \pi_t(S_s^{(n)}(t))) + \beta^{T_F-n} r(S_s^{(n)}(T_F),\cdot)]] \\
&= \max_{\pi^{(n)}}[r(s,\pi_n(s)) + \beta \sum_{S^{(n)}(s)} p(S_s^{(n)} \mid \pi^{(n)}) \\
&\quad \cdot [\sum_{t=n+1}^{T_F-1} \beta^{t-(n+1)} r(S_s^{(n)}(t), \pi_t(S_s^{(n)}(t))) \\
&\quad + \beta^{T_F-(n+1)} r(S_s^{(n)}(T_F),\cdot)]] \\
&= \max_{\pi^{(n)}}[r(s,\pi_n(s)) + \beta \sum_{s'\in S} P_S(s'|s,\pi_n(s)) \sum_{S_{s'}^{(n+1)}} p(S_{s'}^{(n+1)} \mid \pi^{(n)}) \\
&\quad \cdot [\sum_{t=n+1}^{T_F-1} \beta^{t-(n+1)} r(S_{s'}^{(n+1)}(t), \pi_t(S_{s'}^{(n+1)}(t))) \\
&\quad + \beta^{T_F-(n+1)} r(S_{s'}^{(n+1)}(T_F),\cdot)]] \\
&= \max_{a\in A}[r(s,a) + \beta \sum_{s'\in S} P_S(s'|s,a) \max_{\pi^{(n+1)}}[\sum_{S_{s'}^{(n+1)}} p(S_{s'}^{(n+1)} \mid \pi^{(n+1)}) \\
&\quad \cdot [\sum_{t=n+1}^{T_F-1} \beta^{t-(n+1)} r(S_{s'}^{(n+1)}(t), \pi_t(S_{s'}^{(n+1)}(t))) \\
&\quad + \beta^{T_F-(n+1)} r(S_{s'}^{(n+1)}(T_F),\cdot)]]] \\
&= \max_{a\in A}[r(s,a) + \beta \sum_{s'\in S} P_S(s'|s,a) \max_{\pi^{(n+1)}} E[\sum_{t=n+1}^{T_F-1} \beta^{t-(n+1)} r(s_t, \pi_t(s_t)) \\
&\quad + \beta^{T_F-(n+1)} r(s_{T_F},\cdot) \mid s_{n+1} = s']] \\
&= \max_{a\in A}[r(s,a) + \beta \sum_{s'\in S} P_S(s'|s,a) V_{n+1}(s')]
\end{aligned}$$

$\square$

Lemma 2. *Existence of the Information State MDP*
Let $M := (T, S, A, O, P_S, P_O, r)$ be a partially observable Markov decision process. The information state MDP $M_I := (T, I, A, P_I, r_I)$ satisfies the Markov assumption and the model of M_I is well-defined.

Proof. The Markov assumption is trivially satisfied for M_I, since $I_0 \subset I_1 \subset ... \subset I_{t-1} \subset I_t$. Thus, it holds that $p(I_{t+1} \mid I_t, a_t, I_{t-1}, ..., I_1, I_0) = P_I(I_{t+1} \mid I_t, a_t)$. Since all possible next information states I_{t+1} after executing an action $a_t \in A$ correspond to a next observation $o_{t+1} \in O$, it must hold that

$$\sum_{I' \in I} P_I(I_{t+1} = I' \mid I_t, a_t) = \sum_{o \in O} p(o_{t+1} = o \mid I_t, a_t) \tag{A.2}$$
$$= 1$$

The transition model P_I therefore forms a valid probability distribution for every possible action $a_t \in A$. The term $p(o = o_{t+1} \mid I_t, a_t)$ can be computed from the model of the original POMDP M. The same holds for the term $p(s_t = s \mid I_t)$ used to define the reward function r_I. A formal derivation of these quantities is provided by the proof of Theorem 2. □

Lemma 3. *Equivalence of POMDP and Information State MDP*
Let $M := (T, S, A, O, P_S, P_O, r)$ be a partially observable Markov decision process and let $M_I := (T, I, A, P_I, r_I)$ be the corresponding information state MDP. Then, it holds that

$$\pi_I^* \text{ is optimal for } M_I \Leftrightarrow \pi_I^* \text{ is optimal for } M$$

Proof. We assume that the initial information state I_0 is fixed such that the information state space remains countable. However, the provided analyisis can be easily generalized to an uncountable information state space by replacing the sums by integrals.

We only consider the case of an infinite set of time steps T. If T is finite, almost the same arguments hold.

$$E_{\{I_t\}}[\sum_{t=0}^{\infty} \beta^t r^I(I_t, \pi_I^*(I_t))] = \sum_{t=0}^{\infty} \beta^t E_{\{I_t\}}[r^I(I_t, \pi_I^*(I_t))]$$

$$= \sum_{t=0}^{\infty} \beta^t \sum_{I' \in I} p(I_t = I') r^I(I', \pi_I^*(I'))$$

$$= \sum_{t=0}^{\infty} \beta^t \sum_{I' \in I} p(I_t = I') \sum_{s \in S} p(s_t = s \mid I_t = I')$$
$$\cdot r(s, \pi_I^*(I'))$$

$$= \sum_{t=0}^{\infty} \beta^t \sum_{I' \in I} \sum_{s \in S} p(I_t = I') p(s_t = s \mid I_t = I')$$
$$\cdot r(s, \pi_I^*(I'))$$

$$= \sum_{t=0}^{\infty} \beta^t \sum_{I' \in I} \sum_{s \in S} \frac{p(I_t = I') p(s_t = s, I_t = I')}{p(I_t = I')}$$
$$\cdot r(s, \pi_I^*(I'))$$

$$= \sum_{t=0}^{\infty} \beta^t \sum_{I' \in I} \sum_{s \in S} p(s_t = s, I_t = I') r(s, \pi_I^*(I'))$$

$$= \sum_{t=0}^{\infty} \beta^t E_{\{I_t, s_t\}}[r(s_t, \pi_I^*(I_t))]$$

$$= E_{\{I_t, s_t\}}[\sum_{t=0}^{\infty} \beta^t r(s_t, \pi_I^*(I_t))] \qquad (A.3)$$

Since π_I^* is optimal for the MDP M_I, π_I^* maximizes Equation (A.3). Thus, π_I^* is an optimal policy with respect to the POMDP M. □

Lemma 8. *Sufficient History Length for Infinite State Spaces*
Let $M := (T, S, A, O, f_S, f_O, r)$ be a deterministic POMDP such that S is an infinite set of states and O is a finite set of observations. Then, it holds that $l_{su} = \infty$.

Proof. We assume that the sufficient history length l_{su} is a finite constant. Consider a history space $H_{l_{su}} \subset H^*$ containing every possible history list up to length l_{su}. Since there exists an identifying history list no longer than l_{su} for every state, the history space $H_{l_{su}}$ contains at least one such list for every state. Since the state space if of infinite size, the history space $H_{l_{su}}$ must therefore contain an infinite number of history lists. However, given a finite number of observations and a finite number of actions, the number of possible history lists up to a finite length l_{su} is bounded. Thus, also the size of the history space $H_{l_{su}}$ is bounded. This contradiction shows that it must hold $l_{su} = \infty$. □

Lemma 10. *Convergence of Q-Learning with the MaxProb Heuristic*
Let $M := (T, S, A, O, f_S, f_O, r)$ be a deterministic partially observable Markov Decision Process. Let $0 \leq \beta < 1$ a discounting rate and let $H \subset H^*$ be a history space. If the set of valid transition instances $\mathcal{F}^{vl}$ is sampled according to the MaxProb heuristic (Algorithm 11), then every single run of the Q-learning update loop will converge to a unique fixed point.

Proof. Consider a set of sampled transition instances $\mathcal{F}$ before executing a run of the Q-learning update loop from Algorithm 11. The set of valid transitions $\mathcal{F}^{vl}$ is derived from $\mathcal{F}$ by selecting a single transition instance (h, a, r', h') for every history list $h \in H$ and action $a \in A$ occuring in $\mathcal{F}$. We have to show that it is still possible to build a valid deterministic MDP M_H such that the Q-learning updates performed during a single run of the update loop (Algorithm 11) are equivalent to ordinary Q-learning updates on M_H.

The state space S_H of the MDP M_H contains all history lists from H, i.e. $S_H := H$. An action $a \in A$ can be executed from history list $h \in H$ if $a \in A_h^{vl}$, i.e. if the set $\mathcal{F}^{vl}$ contains a transition instance from history list h after executing action a. The transition function f_H of MDP M_H for a pair $(h, a) \in H \times A$ is defined by the transition instance $(h, a, r', h') \in \mathcal{F}^{vl}$ selected by the MaxProb heuristic, i.e. $f_H(h, a) := h'$. Since only a single instance is selected for each pair $(h, a) \in H \times A$, the transition function is well-defined. The same holds for the reward function $r_H(h, a) := r'$. The rest of the proof follows with the same arguments as for the proof of Theorem 6. □

Appendix B

Proofs of Theorems

Theorem 2. *Belief States Form a Sufficient Statistic*
Let $M := (T, S, A, O, P_S, P_O, r)$ be a partially observable Markov decision process and let $M_I := (T, I, A, P_I, r_I)$ be the corresponding information state MDP. If the set of time steps T is finite such that T_F is a maximal element of T, then it is possible to rewrite the optimal value functions V_n^* ($0 \leq n \leq T_F$) in terms of belief states.

$$V_n^*(b) := \max_{a \in A}[\sum_{s \in S} b(s)r(s,a) + \beta \sum_{o \in O} \sum_{s' \in s, s'' \in S} P_O(o \mid s'', a) \quad\quad (B.1)$$
$$\cdot P_S(s'' \mid s', a)b(s')V_{n+1}^*(b_o^a)]$$

The belief state b_o^a denotes the successor belief of b after executing action $a \in A$ and making observation $o \in O$.

$$b_o^a(s) := \frac{P_O(o \mid s, a) \sum_{s' \in S} P_S(s \mid s', a) b(s')}{\sum_{s' \in S, s'' \in S} P_S(s'' \mid s', a) P_O(o \mid s'', a) b(s')} \quad\quad (B.2)$$

The initial value function $V_{T_F}^*$ is given by the expected terminal reward at time T_F.

$$V_{T_F}^*(b) := \sum_{s \in S} b(s) r(s, \cdot) \quad\quad (B.3)$$

Proof. To avoid additional notation, the symbol V_n^* denotes both a value function on information states as well as a value function on belief states. The argument of V_n^* resolves any ambiguities.

Let $b := b_t$ be the current belief state at time t and let $I_{t+1} = \{a_0, o_1, ..., a_t = a, o_{t+1} = o\}$ be the information state at time $t+1$. First, we will prove that the next belief state b_{t+1} is given by b_o^a as defined above.

$$\begin{aligned}
b_{t+1}(s) &= p(s_{t+1} = s \mid I_{t+1}) \\
&= p(s_{t+1} = s \mid I_t, o_{t+1} = o, a_t = a) \\
&= \frac{p(s_{t+1} = s, o_{t+1} = o, I_t, a_t = a)}{p(o_{t+1} = o, I_t, a_t = a)} \\
&= \frac{p(s_{t+1} = s, o_{t+1} = o \mid I_t, a_t = a)}{p(o_{t+1} = o \mid I_t, a_t = a)}
\end{aligned} \qquad (B.4)$$

We will derive the expressions for the numerator and denominator of Equation (B.4) separately. From now on, we will write o for $o_{t+1} = o$ and a for $a_t = a$ using a short hand notation.

$$\begin{aligned}
p(s_{t+1} = s, o \mid I_t, a) &= \sum_{s' \in S} p(o, s_{t+1} = s, s_t = s' \mid I_t, a) \\
&= \sum_{s' \in S} \frac{p(o, s_{t+1} = s, s_t = s', I_t, a)}{p(I_t, a)} \\
&= \sum_{s' \in S} \frac{p(o, s_{t+1} = s, s_t = s', I_t, a) p(I_t, a)}{p(s_{t+1} = s, s_t = s', I_t, a) p(I_t, a)} \\
&\quad \cdot \frac{p(s_{t+1} = s, s_t = s', I_t, a) p(s_t = s', I_t, a)}{p(s_t = s', I_t, a) p(I_t, a)} \\
&= \sum_{s' \in S} p(o \mid s_{t+1} = s, s_t = s', I_t, a) \\
&\quad \cdot p(s_{t+1} = s \mid s_t = s', I_t, a) p(s_t = s' \mid I_t, a) \\
&= \sum_{s' \in S} p(o \mid s_{t+1} = s, a) \\
&\quad \cdot p(s_{t+1} = s \mid s_t = s', a) p(s_t = s' \mid I_t, a) \\
&= P_O(o \mid s, a) \sum_{s' \in S} P_S(s \mid s', a) b(s') \qquad (B.5)
\end{aligned}$$

$$
\begin{aligned}
p(o \mid I_t, a) &= \frac{p(o, I_t, a)}{p(I_t, a)} \\
&= \sum_{s'' \in S, s' \in S} \frac{p(o, s_{t+1} = s'', s_t = s', I_t, a)}{p(I_t, a)} \\
&= \sum_{s'' \in S, s' \in S} \frac{p(o, s_{t+1} = s'', s_t = s', I_t, a) p(s_t = s' \mid I_t, a)}{p(s_t = s', I_t, a)} \\
&= \sum_{s'' \in S, s' \in S} p(o, s_{t+1} = s'', s_t = s', I_t, a) p(s_t = s' \mid I_t, a) \\
&\quad \cdot \frac{p(s_{t+1} = s'' \mid s_t = s', I_t, a)}{p(s_{t+1} = s'', s_t = s', I_t, a)} \\
&= \sum_{s'' \in s, s' \in S} p(o, s_{t+1} = s'', s_t = s', I_t, a) \\
&\quad \cdot p(s_t = s' \mid I_t, a) p(s_{t+1} = s'' \mid s_t = s', I_t, a) \\
&\quad \cdot \frac{p(o \mid s_{t+1} = s'', s_t = s', I_t, a)}{p(o, s_{t+1} = s'', s_t = s', I_t, a)} \\
&= \sum_{s'' \in s, s' \in S} p(s_t = s' \mid I_t, a) p(s_{t+1} = s'' \mid s_t = s', I_t, a) \\
&\quad \cdot P(o \mid s_{t+1} = s'', s_t = s', I_t, a) \\
&= \sum_{s'' \in s, s' \in S} p(s_t = s' \mid I_t) p(s_{t+1} = s'' \mid s_t = s', a) \\
&\quad \cdot P(o \mid s_{t+1} = s'', a) \\
&= \sum_{s'' \in s, s' \in S} P_S(s'' \mid s', a) P_O(o \mid s'', a) b(s') \quad \text{(B.6)}
\end{aligned}
$$

To derive the expressions (B.4), (B.5), and (B.6), we have only used the definitions of conditional probability, the sum rule of probability and the Markov assumption.

To prove that the optimal value functions V_n^*, $(0 \leq n \leq T_F)$ can be rewritten in terms of belief states, we introduce a mapping $g : I \to B$ from information states to belief states such that $g(I') := b'$ with $b'(s) := p(s \mid I')$. The proof consists of verifying the following two propositions:

1. $\forall t \in T : b_t = g(I_t)$

2. $\forall t \in T : V_n^*(I_t) = V_n^*(g(I_t))$

The first proposition follows immediately from $b_0 = I_0$ and the definition of the belief state b_t (Definition 12).

The second proposition follows by induction over n. If $n = T_F$, then it holds that

$$V_{T_F}^*(I_t) = \sum_{s \in S} p(s_t = s \mid I_t) r(s, \cdot)$$
$$= \sum_{s \in S} b_t(s) r(s, \cdot)$$
$$= V_{T_F}^*(g(I_t))$$

Now we will show that it holds $\forall t \in T : V_n^*(I_t) = V_n^*(g(I_t))$ assuming that $\forall t \in T : V_{n+1}^*(I_t) = V_{n+1}^*(g(I_t))$. Since $b_t = g(I_t)$, it is sufficient to show $\forall t \in T : V_n^*(I_t) = V_n^*(b_t)$ assuming that $\forall t \in T : V_{n+1}^*(I_t) = V_{n+1}^*(b_t)$.

$$V_n^*(I_t) = \max_{a \in A} [\sum_{s \in S} p(s_t = s \mid I_t) r(s, a) + \beta \sum_{o \in O} p(o_{t+1} = o \mid I_t, a) V_{n+1}^*(I_{t+1})]$$
$$= \max_{a \in A} [\sum_{s \in S} p(s_t = s \mid I_t) r(s, a) + \beta \sum_{o \in O} p(o_{t+1} = o \mid I_t, a) V_{n+1}^*(b_{t+1})]$$
$$= \max_{a \in A} [\sum_{s \in S} b_t(s) r(s, a) + \beta \sum_{o \in O} p(o_{t+1} = o \mid I_t, a) V_{n+1}^*(b_o^a)]$$
$$= \max_{a \in A} [\sum_{s \in S} b_t(s) r(s, a) + \beta \sum_{o \in O} \sum_{s' \in S, s'' \in S} P_O(o \mid s'', a)$$
$$\cdot P_S(s'' \mid s', a) b_t(s') V_{n+1}^*(b_o^a)]$$
$$= V_n^*(b_t)$$

In the fourth equation, we replaced the term $p(_{t+1} = o \mid I_t, a)$ by the right side of Equation (B.6). $\qquad\square$

Theorem 3. *Compact Representation of the Value Function*
Let $M := (T, S, A, O, P_S, P_O, r)$ be a partially observable Markov decision process. If the set of time steps T is finite such that $T_F \in T$ is a maximal element of T, then the optimal value functions V_n^* ($0 \leq t \leq T_F$) with respect to M are piecewise linear and convex. Moreover, V_n^* can be represented by a finite set of vectors Γ_n such that $V_n^*(b) = \max_{\gamma \in \Gamma_n} b * \gamma$. The $*$ symbol denotes the dot product of two vectors. The set Γ_{T_F} consists of the single vector $R(s) := r(s, \cdot)$. For $0 \leq n < T_F$, it holds that

$$\Gamma_n := \{\sum_{o \in O} \alpha_{f(o)}^{o,a} \mid f \in f(O, \Gamma_{n+1}), a \in A\}$$

$$\forall \gamma \in \Gamma_{n+1} : \alpha_\gamma^{o,a}(s') := \frac{r(s', a)}{|O|} + \beta \sum_{s \in S} P_O(o \mid s, a) P_S(s \mid s', a) \gamma(s)$$

The symbol $f(O, \Gamma_{n+1})$ denotes the set of possible mappings from observations to vectors from Γ_{n+1}.

Proof. We will only prove that the value functions V_n^* can be represented by a set of vectors. The arguments for proving the convexity and the piecewise linearity of the value function can be found in in [SS73].

First, we will again state the value iteration algorithm on belief states. For $0 \leq n < T_F$, it holds that

$$V_n^*(b) = \max_{a \in A}[\sum_{s' \in S} b(s') r(s', a) + \beta \sum_{o \in O} \sum_{s' \in S, s'' \in S} P_O(o \mid s'', a) \\ \cdot P_S(s'' \mid s', a) b(s') V_{n+1}^*(b_o^a)] \quad (B.7)$$

The belief state b_o^a denotes the successor belief of b after executing action $a \in A$ and making observation $o \in O$. The value iteration algorithm consists of computing the values for all belief states by iterating Equation (B.7).

We will make use of an inductive argument. If $n = T_F$, then there is no decision left. For this special case, the expected terminal reward is given by $V_{T_F}^*(b) = \sum_{s \in S} b(s) r(s, \cdot)$. Thus, the value function $V_{T_F}^*$ can be represented by a sinlge vector $R(s) := r(s, \cdot)$. It is easy to see that $V_{T_F}^*(b) = b * R$.

If $n < T_F$, we consider the problem of representing V_n^* as a set of vectors given that V_{n+1}^* is already in the desired form. Let Γ_{n+1} be a set of vectors such that $V_{n+1}^*(b) = \max_{\gamma \in \Gamma_{n+1}} b * \gamma$. For convenience, we will write the reward function as a vector $R^a(s) := r(s, a)$. We now reinsert V_{n+1}^* into Equation (B.7).

$$V_n^*(b) = \max_{a \in A}[b * R^a + \beta \sum_{o \in O} \sum_{s' \in S, s'' \in S} P_O(o \mid s'', a) \\ \cdot P_S(s'' \mid s', a) b(s') \max_{\gamma \in \Gamma_{n+1}}[b_a^o * \gamma]]$$

$$= \max_{a \in A}[b * R^a + \beta \sum_{o \in O} \max_{\gamma \in \Gamma_{n+1}}[\sum_{s' \in s, s'' \in S} P_O(o \mid s'', a) \\ \cdot P_S(s'' \mid s', a) b(s') \sum_{s \in S} b_o^a(s) \gamma(s)]] \quad (B.8)$$

Consider the term
$$B := \sum_{s' \in s, s'' \in S} P_O(o \mid s'', a) P_S(s'' \mid s', a) b(s') \sum_{s \in S} b_o^a(s) \gamma(s)$$

If we replace b_o^a by the right side of Equation (B.2), then the double sum over states in B cancels out. It holds that

$$B = \sum_{s' \in s, s'' \in S} P_O(o \mid s'', a) P_S(s'' \mid s', a) b(s') \sum_{s \in S} b_a^o(s) \gamma(s)$$
$$= \sum_{s \in S} P_O(o \mid s, a) \sum_{s' \in S} P_S(s \mid s', a) b(s') \gamma(s)$$

If we reinsert term B into Equation (B.8), we get the following equations:

$$V_n^*(b) = \max_{a \in A}[b * R^a + \beta \sum_{o \in O} \max_{\gamma \in \Gamma_{n+1}} [\sum_{s \in S} P_O(o \mid s, a)$$
$$\cdot \sum_{s' \in S} P_S(s \mid s', a) b(s') \gamma(s)]]$$
$$= \max_{a \in A}[b * R^a + \beta \sum_{o \in O} \max_{\gamma \in \Gamma_{n+1}} [\sum_{s' \in S} \sum_{s \in S} P_O(o \mid s, a)$$
$$\cdot P_S(s \mid s', a) \gamma(s) b(s')]]$$
$$= \max_{a \in A}[\sum_{o \in O} \max_{\gamma \in \Gamma_{n+1}} [\sum_{s' \in S} (\frac{r(s', a)}{|O|} + \beta \sum_{s \in S} P_O(o \mid s, a)$$
$$\cdot P_S(s \mid s', a) \gamma(s)) b(s')]] \tag{B.9}$$

Let for all observations $o \in O$, actions $a \in A$ and vectors $\gamma \in \Gamma_{n+1}$, the vector $\alpha_\gamma^{o,a}$ be defined as

$$\alpha_\gamma^{o,a}(s') := \frac{r(s', a)}{|O|} + \beta \sum_{s \in S} P_O(o \mid s, a) P_S(s \mid s', a) \gamma(s) \tag{B.10}$$

It follows that

$$V_n^*(b) = \max_{a \in A}[\sum_{o \in O} \max_{\gamma \in \Gamma_{n+1}} [\sum_{s' \in S} \alpha_\gamma^{o,a}(s') b(s')]]$$
$$= \max_{a \in A}[\sum_{o \in O} \max_{\gamma \in \Gamma_{n+1}} [\alpha_\gamma^{o,a} * b]] \tag{B.11}$$

Now we can define the new set of vectors for value function V_n^*. Given an action $a \in A$ and a mapping $f : O \to \Gamma_{n+1}$, the vector $\gamma_{f,a}$ is defined as $\gamma_{f,a} := \sum_{o \in O} \alpha_{f(o)}^{o,a}$. Let $f(O, \Gamma_{n+1})$ denote the set of all possible mappings from observations to Γ_{n+1}-vectors. The value function V_n^* is then equivalent to the maximal dot product of all possible vectors $\gamma_{f,a}$ and a belief state b.

$$V_n^*(b) = \max_{f \in f(O, \Gamma_{n+1}), a \in A} b * \gamma_{f,a} \tag{B.12}$$

It follows that

$$\begin{aligned}\Gamma_n &= \{\gamma_{f,a} \mid f \in f(O, \Gamma_{n+1}), a \in A\} \\ &= \{\sum_{o \in O} \alpha^{o,a}_{f(o)} \mid f \in f(O, \Gamma_{n+1}), a \in A\}\end{aligned} \quad (\text{B.13})$$

□

Theorem 7. *Detection of Identifying History Lists with Criterion CC*
Let $H \subset H^*$ be a history space and let $h \in H$ be a history list of length $\hat{k} := |h|$. If $k - \hat{k} \geq l_{su}$ for a fixed $k \in \mathbb{N}$, then the following two propositions hold:

H is k-complete : h is identifying $\Rightarrow \nexists h' \in H : h' \neq h$, h is a suffix of h'
(If H is k-complete, then criterion CC is complete)

H satisfies 4.1-2 : h is identifying $\Leftarrow \nexists h' \in H : h' \neq h$, h is a suffix of h'
(If H satisfies the conditions (4.1) and (4.2), then criterion CC is correct)

Proof. ($\Rightarrow$):
Let $h \in H$ be an identifying history list and let $h^{id^*} \in H^*$ be the minimal identifying suffix of h. Since $|h^{id^*}| \leq |h| = \hat{k} \leq k - l_{su}$, it holds that $h^{id^*} \in H^{id^*}_{k-l_{su}}$. Since h^{id^*} is also a suffix of h, it follows from condition (4.3) that $h = h^{id^*}$. Thus, it holds that $h \in H^{id^*}_{k-l_{su}}$ and it follows again from condition (4.3) that there is no history list $h' \in H$ such that $h \neq h'$ and h is a suffix of h'.
($\Leftarrow$):
Let $[s_0, a_0, ..., s_{t-\hat{k}}, a_{t-\hat{k}}, ..., a_{t-1}, s_t]$ be a sequence of states and actions generated by the transition model f_S. Let $[o_0, a_0, ..., o_{t-\hat{k}}, a_{t-\hat{k}}, ..., a_{t-1}, o_t]$ be the corresponding sequence of observations and actions generated by the observation model f_O. We assume that $h = [o_{(t-\hat{k})+1}, a_{(t-\hat{k})+1}, ..., a_{t-1}, o_t]$ is a suffix of the sequence with $|h| = \hat{k}$. We assume further that h is a non-identifying history list. We have to show that there is at least one history list in H containing h as a suffix. By the definition of the sufficient history length l_{su}, there exists an identifying history list $h' \in H^*$, $h' := [o'_0, a'_0, ..., a'_{r-2}, o'_{r-1}]$ for state $s_{t-\hat{k}}$ with $r \leq l_{su}$. Consider the history list $h'' := [o'_0, a'_0, ..., o'_{r-1} = o_{(t-\hat{k})+1}, a_{(t-\hat{k})+1}, ..., a_{t-1}, o_t]$, which is built by extending h' with history list h (at the tail). The first thing to show is that $h'' \in H^*$, i.e. the history list h'' can be generated by the transition model f_S and the observation model f_O. Since h' is an identifying history list for state $s_{t-\hat{k}}$, it trivially holds that $h' \in H^*$. We assumed that the sequence $h = [o_{(t-\hat{k})+1}, a_{(t-\hat{k})+1}, ..., a_{t-1}, o_t]$ can be generated from state $s_{t-\hat{k}}$ by the transition model f_s and the observation model f_O. The observations o'_{r-1} and $o_{(t-\hat{k})+1}$ must therefore be the same, since both observations are made of state $s_{t-\hat{k}}$. Since h'' is a concatenation of history list h' and history list h, it must hold that $h'' \in H^*$. It follows from Lemma 5 that h'' is an identifying history list for state s_t, because h'' is an extension of the identifying history list h'. Let h^{id^*} be the minimal identifying suffix of h''. Since both h^{id^*} and h are a suffix of h'', it must hold that either h is a suffix of h^{id^*} or h^{id^*} is a suffix of h. If h^{id^*} is a suffix of h (including the case $h = h^{id^*}$), then it follows from Lemma 4 that h is an identifying history list. This would be a contradiction to our assumption that h is a non-identifying history list. Thus, it must hold that h is a suffix of h^{id^*} with $h \neq h^{id^*}$. If $|h^{id^*}| \leq k - l_{su}$, then it holds that $h^{id^*} \in H^{id^*}_{k-l_{su}}$ and it follows from condition (4.1) that $h^{id^*} \in H$. In this case, we are finished, since h is a suffix of h^{id^*}. If $|h^{id^*}| > k - l_{su}$, then h^{id^*} has a length

of at most k, because $|h| = \hat{k}, |h'| \le l_{su}, |h''| = |h| + |h'| - 1$ and $k \ge \hat{k} + l_{su}$. Thus, it holds that $h^{id^*} \in H_k^{id^*} \setminus H_{k-l_{su}}^{id^*}$. It follows from condition (4.2) that there exists a suffix $h''' \in H$ of h^{id^*} with $|h'''| > k - l_{su}$. Since h is a suffix of h^{id^*} and $|h| < |h'''|$, h must be a suffix of h''' with $h \ne h'''$. Thus, we found a history list in H containing h as a suffix. □

Appendix C

Learning Curves for Criterion CC

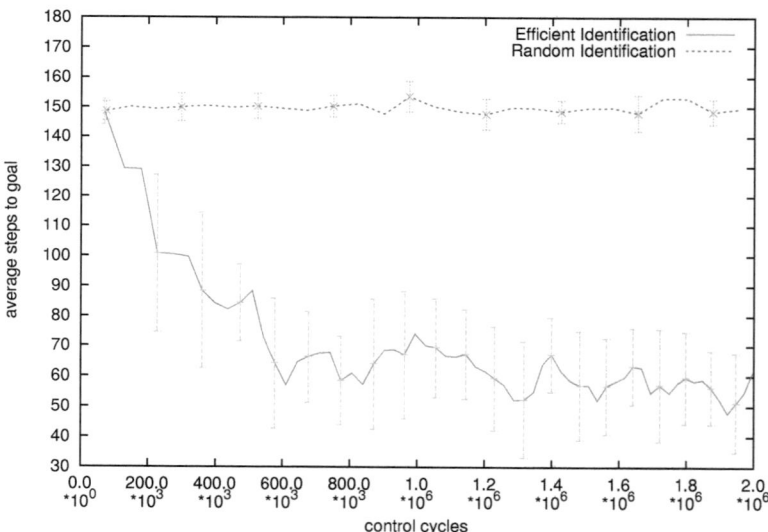

Figure C.1: The Identify&Exploit algorithm applied to the big maze using criterion CC. The x-axis shows the number of control cycles, while the y-axis shows the number of steps to the goal averaged over all possible starting states. Setting of parameters: 6-complete history space, constant exploration rate $\epsilon = 0.2$, discounting rate $\beta = 1.0$, and the maximal search depth $L = 7$ (efficient identification). After every $|\mathcal{F}_{new}| = 100000$ sampled transition instances, the Q-learning update loop was executed.

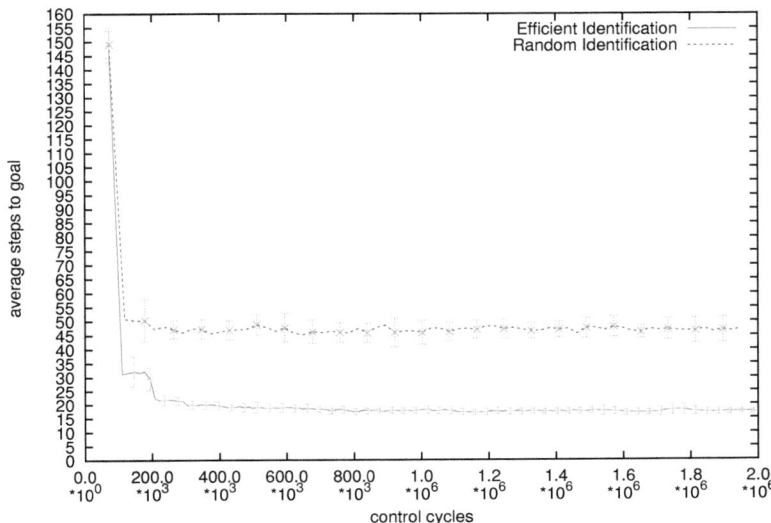

Figure C.2: The Identify&Exploit algorithm applied to the big maze using criterion CC. The x-axis shows the number of control cycles, while the y-axis shows the number of steps to the goal averaged over all possible starting states. Setting of parameters: 7-complete history space, constant exploration rate $\epsilon = 0.1$, discounting rate $\beta = 1.0$, and the maximal search depth $L = 4$ (efficient identification). After every $|\mathcal{F}_{new}| = 100000$ sampled transition instances, the Q-learning update loop was executed.

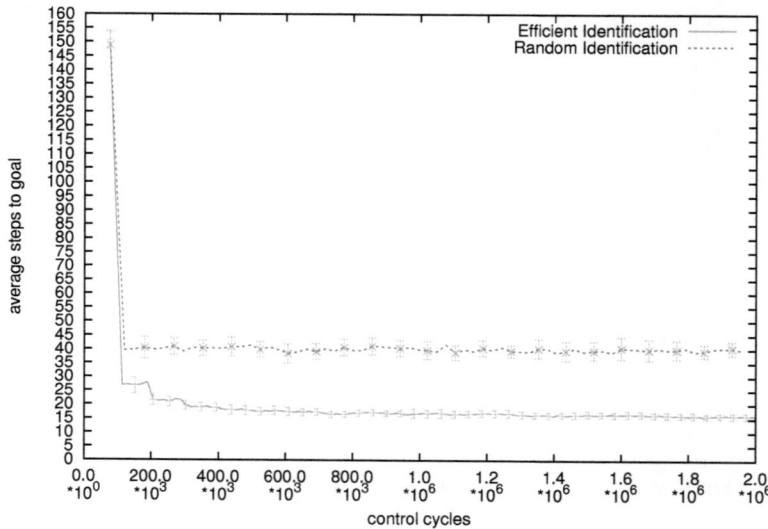

Figure C.3: The Identify&Exploit algorithm applied to the big maze using criterion CC. The x-axis shows the number of control cycles, while the y-axis shows the number of steps to the goal averaged over all possible starting states. Setting of parameters: 8-complete history space, constant exploration rate $\epsilon = 0.2$, discounting rate $\beta = 1.0$, and the maximal search depth $L = 3$ (efficient identification). After every $|\mathcal{F}_{new}| = 100000$ sampled transition instances, the Q-learning update loop was executed.

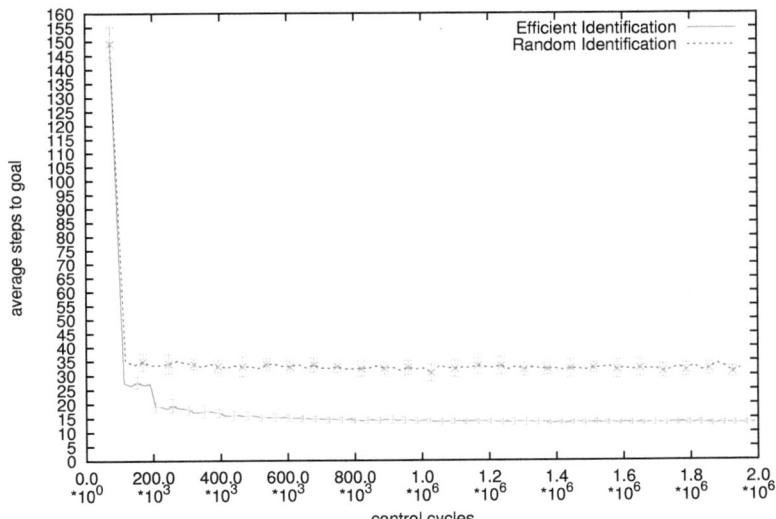

Figure C.4: The Identify&Exploit algorithm applied to the big maze using criterion CC. The x-axis shows the number of control cycles, while the y-axis shows the number of steps to the goal averaged over all possible starting states. Setting of parameters: 9-complete history space, constant exploration rate $\epsilon = 0.2$, discounting rate $\beta = 1.0$, and the maximal search depth $L = 2$ (efficient identification). After every $|\mathcal{F}_{new}| = 100000$ sampled transition instances, the Q-learning update loop was executed.

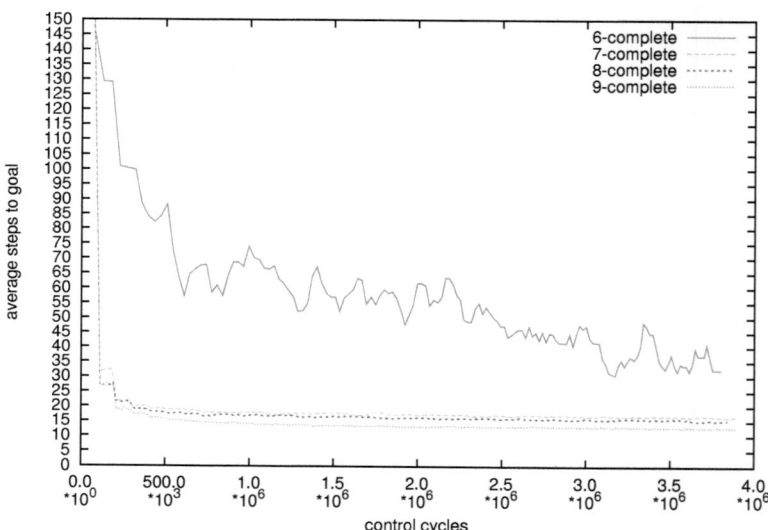

Figure C.5: The Identify&Exploit algorithm applied to the big maze using the efficient identification strategy and criterion CC. The x-axis shows the number of control cycles, while the y-axis shows the number of steps to the goal averaged over all possible starting states.

Appendix D

Learning Curves for Criterion CE

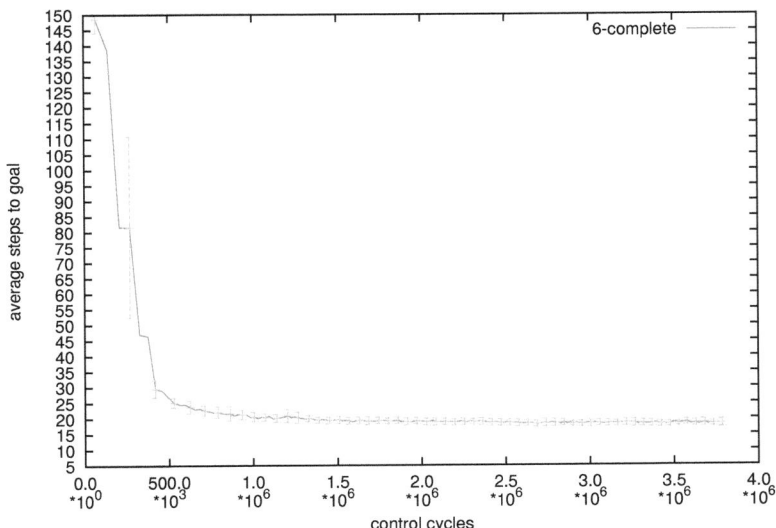

Figure D.1: The Identify&Exploit algorithm applied to the big maze using criterion CE. The x-axis shows the number of control cycles, while the y-axis shows the number of steps to the goal averaged over all possible starting states. Setting of parameters: 6-complete history space, constant exploration rate $\epsilon = 0.2$, discounting rate $\beta = 0.98$, and the maximal search depth $L = 3$ (efficient identification). After every $|\mathcal{F}| = 100000$ sampled transition instances, the Q-learning update loop was executed.

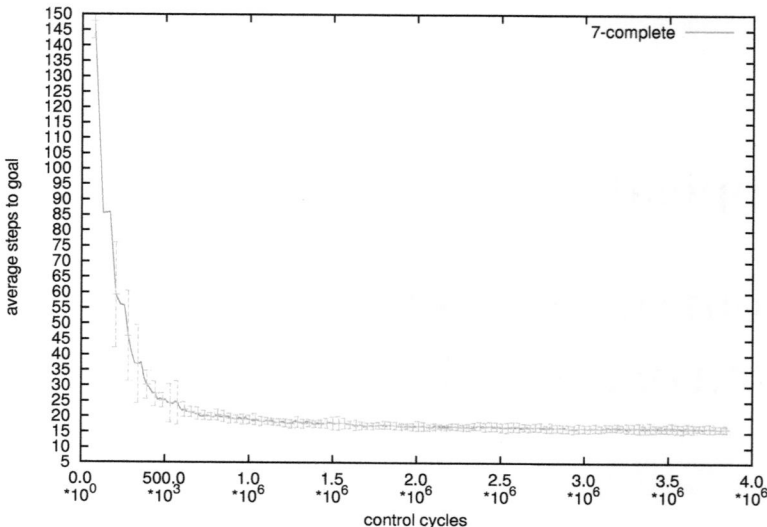

Figure D.2: The Identify&Exploit algorithm applied to the big maze using criterion CE. The x-axis shows the number of control cycles, while the y-axis shows the number of steps to the goal averaged over all possible starting states. Setting of parameters: 7-complete history space, constant exploration rate $\epsilon = 0.1$, discounting rate $\beta = 0.98$, and the maximal search depth $L = 3$ (efficient identification). After every $|\mathcal{F}| = 100000$ sampled transition instances, the Q-learning update loop was executed.

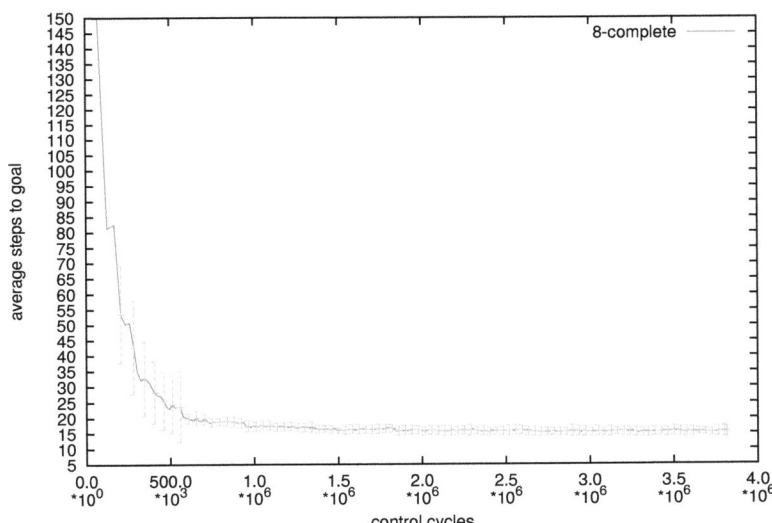

Figure D.3: The Identify&Exploit algorithm applied to the big maze using criterion CE. The x-axis shows the number of control cycles, while the y-axis shows the number of steps to the goal averaged over all possible starting states. Setting of parameters: 8-complete history space, constant exploration rate $\epsilon = 0.2$, discounting rate $\beta = 0.98$, and the maximal search depth $L = 3$ (efficient identification). After every $|\mathcal{F}| = 100000$ sampled transition instances, the Q-learning update loop was executed.

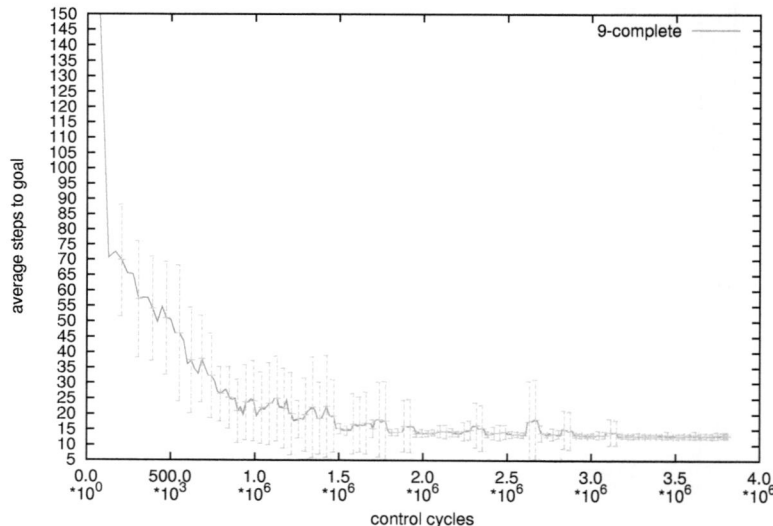

Figure D.4: The Identify&Exploit algorithm applied to the big maze using criterion CE. The x-axis shows the number of control cycles, while the y-axis shows the number of steps to the goal averaged over all possible starting states. Setting of parameters: 9-complete history space, constant exploration rate $\epsilon = 0.2$, discounting rate $\beta = 0.98$, and the maximal search depth $L = 2$ (efficient identification). After every $|\mathcal{F}| = 100000$ sampled transition instances, the Q-learning update loop was executed.

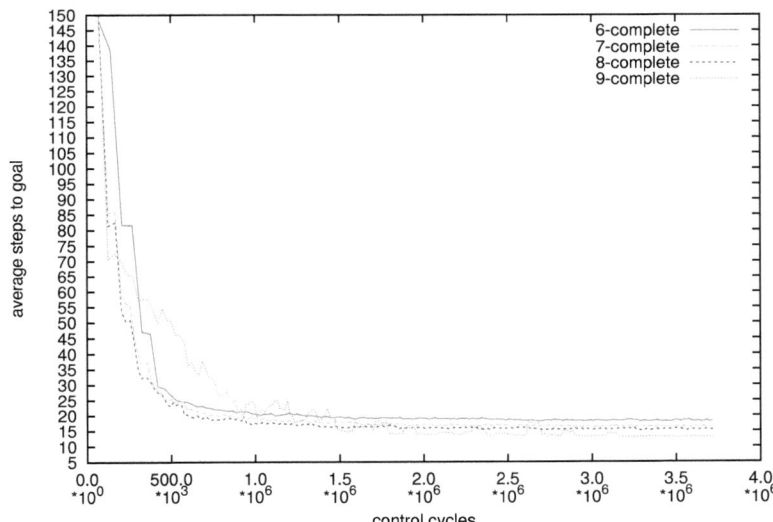

Figure D.5: The Identify&Exploit algorithm applied to the big maze using the efficient identification strategy and criterion CE. The x-axis shows the number of control cycles, while the y-axis shows the number of steps to the goal averaged over all possible starting states.

Bibliography

[Bak01]   Bram Bakker. Reinforcement learning with long short-term memory. In *Proceedings of the 14th Conference on Neural Information Processing Systems (NIPS)*, pages 1475–1482, 2001.

[BB04]   Darius Braziunas and Craig Boutilier. Stochastic local search for pomdp controllers. In *Proceedings of 19th National Conference on Artificial Intelligence (AAAI)*, pages 690–696, 2004.

[Ber01]   Dimitri P. Bertsekas. *Dynamic Programming And Optimal Control*, volume Two-Volume Set. Athena Scientific, second edition, 2001.

[BG98]   Blai Bonet and Héctor Geffner. Learning sorting and decision trees with pomdps. In *Proceedings of the 15th International Conference on Machine Learning (ICML)*, pages 73–81, 1998.

[Bos98]   Karl Bosch. *Statistik-Taschenbuch*. R. Oldenbourg Verlag, 1998.

[BP96]   Craig Boutilier and David Poole. Computing optimal policies for partially observable decision processes using compact representations. In *Proceedings of the 13th National Conference on Artificial Intelligence (AAAI)*, pages 1168–1175. AAAI Press / The MIT Press, 1996.

[BPSW70] Leonard E. Baum, Ted Petrie, George Soules, and Norman Weiss. A maximization technique occuring in the statistical analysis of probabilistic functiions markov chains. *Annals of Mathematical Statistics*, 41(1):164–171, 1970.

[Bra97]   Ronen I. Brafman. A heuristic variable grid solution method for pomdps. In *Proceedings of the 14th National Conference on Artificial Intelligence (AAAI)*, 1997.

[BSA83]   Andrew Barto, Richard Sutton, and Charles Anderson. Neuron-like elements that can solve difficult learning control problems. In *IEEE. Trans. on Systems, Man and Cybernetics*, volume 13, pages 835–846, 1983.

[BT96] Dimitri P. Bertsekas and John N. Tsisiklis. *Neuro-Dynamic Programming*. Athena Scientific, 1996.

[Che88] Hsien-Te Cheng. *Algorithms for Partially Observable Markov Decision Processes*. PhD thesis, University of British Columbia, Canada, 1988.

[Chr92] Lonnie Chrisman. Reinforcement learning with perceptual aliasing: The perceptual distinctions approach. In *Proceedings of the 10th National Conference on Artificial Intelligence (AAAI)*, pages 183–188, 1992.

[CLZ97] Anthony R. Cassandra, Michael L. Littman, and Nevin L. Zhang. Incremental pruning: A simple, fast, exact method for pomdps. In *Proceedings of the 13th Conference on Uncertainty in Artificial Intelligence (UAI)*, pages 54–61, 1997.

[DG97] Thomas Dean and Robert Givan. Model minimization in markov decision processes. In *Proceedings of the 14th National Conference on Artificial Intelligence (AAAI)*, pages 106–111, 1997.

[Die00] Thomas G. Dietterich. Hierarchical Reinforcement Learning with the MAXQ Value Function Decomposition. *Journal of Artificial Intelligence Research*, 13:227–303, 2000.

[DRB98] Saso Dzeroski, Luc De Raedt, and Hendrik Blockeel. Relational reinforcement learning. In *Proceedings of the International Workshop on Inductive Logic Programming*, pages 11–22, 1998.

[EGW05] Damien Ernst, Pierre Geurts, and Louis Wehenkel. Tree-based batch mode reinforcement learning. *Journal of Machine Learning Research*, 6:503–556, 2005.

[GDR03] Thomas Gärtner, Kurt Driessens, and Jan Ramon. Graph kernels and gaussian processes for relational reinforcement learning. In *Proceedings of the 13th International Conference on Inductive Logic Programming (ILP)*, pages 146–163, 2003.

[GS05] Faustino J. Gomez and Jürgen Schmidhuber. Co-evolving recurrent neurons learn deep memory pomdps. In *Proceedings of the Conference on Genetic and Evolutionary Computation (GECCO)*, pages 491–498, 2005.

[Han98] Eric A. Hansen. Solving pomdps by searching in policy space. In *Proceedings of the 14th Conference on Uncertainty in Artificial Intelligence (UAI)*, pages 211–219, 1998.

[Hau00] Milos Hauskrecht. Value-function approximations for partially observable markov decision processes. *Journal of Machine Learning Research*, 13:33–94, 2000.

[HJ06]   Michael P. Holmes and Charles Lee Isbell Jr. Looping suffix tree-based inference of partially observable hidden state. In *Proceedings of the 23th International Conference on Machine Learning (ICML)*, pages 409–416, 2006.

[IM98]   Leemon C. Baird III and Andrew W. Moore. Gradient descent for general reinforcement learning. In *Proceedings of the 11th Conference on Neural Information Processing Systems (NIPS)*, pages 968–974, 1998.

[JSJ94]   Tommi Jaakkola, Satinder P. Singh, and Michael I. Jordan. Reinforcement learning algorithm for partially observable markov decision problems. In *Proceedings of the 7th Conference on Neural Information Processing Systems (NIPS)*, pages 345–352, 1994.

[KLC96]   Leslie P. Kaelbling, Michael L. Littman, and Anthony R. Cassandra. Planning and acting in partially observable stochastic domains. Technical Report CS-96-08, Brown Universiy, 1996.

[LCK95]   Michael L. Littman, Anthony R. Cassandra, and Leslie P. Kaelbling. Efficient dynamic-programming updates in partially observable markov decision processes. Technical Report CS-95-19, Brown University, 1995.

[Lit94]   Michael L. Littman. Memoryless policies: Theoretical limitations and practical results. In Dave Cliff, Philip Husbands, Jean-Arcady Meyer, and Stewart W. Wilson, editors, *From Animals to Animats 3: Proceedings of the Third International Conference on Simulation of Adaptive Behavior*, Cambridge, MA, 1994. The MIT Press.

[LM92]   Long-Ji Lin and Tom Mitchell. Memory approaches to reinforcement learning in non markovian domains. Technical Report CMU-CS-92-138, School of Computer Science, Carnegie Mellon University, 1992.

[LP03]   Michail G. Lagoudakis and Ronald Parr. Least-squares policy iteration. *Journal of Machine Learning Research*, 4:1107–1149, 2003.

[LR02]   Martin Lauer and Martin Riedmiller. Generalisation in reinforcement learning and the use of observations-based learning. In *Proceedings of the FGML Workshop*, pages 100–107. G. Kokai and J. Zeidler (eds.), 2002.

[LS98]   John Loch and Satinder P. Singh. Using eligibility traces to find the best memoryless policy in partially observable markov decision processes. In *Proceedings of the 15th International Conference on Machine Learning (ICML)*, pages 323–331, 1998.

[LSS02]   Michael Littman, Richard Sutton, and Satinder Singh. Predictive representations of state. In *Proceedings of the 14th International Conference on Neural Information Processing Systems (NIPS)*, pages 1555–1561, 2002.

[MA93] Andrew W. Moore and Christopher G. Atkeson. Prioritized sweeping: Reinforcement learning with less data and less time. *Machine Learning*, 13:103–130, 1993.

[McC93] Andrew McCallum. Overcoming incomplete perception with util distinction memory. In *Proceedings of the 10th International Conference on Machine Learning (ICML)*, pages 190–196, 1993.

[McC94] Andrew McCallum. Instance-based state identification for reinforcement learning. In *Proceedings of the 7th Conference on Neural Information Processing Systems (NIPS)*, pages 377–384, 1994.

[McC95] Andrew McCallum. Instance-based utile distinctions for reinforcement learning with hidden state. In *Proceedings of the 12th International Conference on Machine Learning (ICML)*, pages 387–395, 1995.

[Mit97] Tom M. Mitchell. *Machine Learning*. McGraw-Hill, 1997.

[MKKC99] Nicolas Meuleau, Kee-Eung Kim, Leslie Pack Kaelbling, and Anthony R. Cassandra. Solving pomdps by searching the space of finite policies. In *Proceedings of the 15th Conference on Uncertainty in Artificial Intelligence (UAI)*, pages 417–426, 1999.

[MM02] Remi Munos and Andrew Moore. Variable resolution discretization in optimal control. *Machine Learning*, 49(2/3):291–323, 2002.

[Moo95] Andrew W. Moore. The parti-game algorithm for variable resolution reinforcement learning in multidimensional state spaces. *Machine Learning*, 21, 1995.

[MPKK99] Nicolas Meuleau, Leonid Peshkin, Kee-Eung Kim, and Leslie Pack Kaelbling. Learning finite-state controllers for partially observable environments. In *Proceedings of the 15th Conference on Uncertainty in Artificial Intelligence (UAI)*, pages 427–436, 1999.

[PB04] Pascal Poupart and Craig Boutilier. Bounded finite state controllers. In *Proceedings of the 15th Conference on Advances in Neural Information Processing Systems (NIPS)*, 2004.

[Pea89] Barak A. Pearlmutter. Learning state space trajectories in recurrent neural networks. *Neural Computation*, 1:263–269, 1989.

[PGT03] Joelle Pineau, Geoffrey Gordon, and Sebastian Thrun. Point-based value iteration: An anytime algorithm for pomdps. In *Proceedings of the International Joint Conference on Artificial Intelligence (IJCAI)*, 2003.

[PMK99] Leonid Peshkin, Nicolas Meuleau, and Leslie Pack Kaelbling. Learning policies with external memory. In *Proceedings of the 16th International Conference on Machine Learning (ICML)*, pages 307–314, 1999.

[PR97] Ronald Parr and Stuart Russel. Reinforcement learning with hierarchies of machines. In *Proceedings of the 10th Conference on Advances in Neural Information Processing Systems (NIPS)*, 1997.

[PVS05] Jan Peters, Sethu Vijayakumar, and Stefan Schaal. Natural actor-critic. In *Proceedings of the 16th European Conference on Machine Learning (ECML)*, pages 280–291, 2005.

[Rey00] Stuart Reynolds. Adaptive resolution model-free reinforcement learning: Decision boundary partitioning. In *Proceedings of the 17th International Conference on Machine Learning (ICML)*, pages 783–790, 2000.

[RF87] Anthony J. Robinson and Frank Fallside. The utility driven dynamic error propagation network. Technical Report CUED/F-INFENG/TR.1, Cambridge University, Engineering Department, 1987.

[Rie05] Martin Riedmiller. Neural fitted q iteration - first experiences with a data efficient neural reinforcement learning method. In *Procedings of the 16th European Conference on Machine Learning (ECML)*, pages 317–328, 2005.

[RN03] Stuart Russel and Peter Norvig. *Artificial Intelligence: A Modern Approach*. Prentice Hall, second edition, 2003.

[RS94] Ronald L. Rivest and Robert E. Schapire. Diversity-based inference of finite automata. *Journal of the Association for Computing Machinery*, 43:555–589, 1994.

[SB98] Richard Sutton and Andrew Barto. *Reinforcement Learning: An Introduction*. MIT Press, Cambridge, Massachusetts, 1998.

[SJJ94] Satinder P. Singh, Tommi Jaakkola, and Michael I. Jordan. Learning without state-estimation in partially observable markovian decision processes. In *Proceedings of the 11th International Conference on Machine Learning (ICML)*, pages 84–292, 1994.

[SMSM99] Richard S. Sutton, David A. McAllester, Satinder P. Singh, and Yishay Mansour. Policy gradient methods for reinforcement learning with function wapproximation. In *Proceedings of the 12th Conference on Neural Information Processing Systems (NIPS)*, pages 1057–1063, 1999.

[Son78]   Edward J. Sondik. The optimal control of partially observable markov processes over the infinite horizon: Discounted costs. *Operations Research*, 26(2):282–304, 1978.

[SPS99]   Richard Sutton, Doina Precup, and Satinder Singh. Between mdps and semi-MDPs: A framework for temporal abstraction in reinforcement learning. *Artificial Intelligence*, 112(1-2):181–211, 1999.

[SR02]   Ralf Schoknecht and Martin A. Riedmiller. Speeding-up reinforcement learning with multi-step actions. In *Proceedings of the 12thInternational Conference on Artificial Neural Networks (ICANN)*, pages 813–818, 2002.

[SR03]   Ralf Schoknecht and Martin Riedmiller. Reinforcement learning on explicitly specified time scales. *Neural Computing and Applications*, 12(2):61–80, 2003.

[SS73]   Richard D. Smallwood and Edward J. Sondik. The optimal control of partially observable markov processes over a finite horizon. *Operations Research*, 21:1071–1088, 1973.

[SS96]   Satinder P. Singh and Richard S. Sutton. Reinforcement learning with replacing eligibility traces. *Machine Learning*, 22(1–3):123–158, 1996.

[Sut96]   Richard S. Sutton. Generalization in reinforcement learning: Successful examples using sparse coarse coding. In *Proceedings of the 9th Conference on Advances in Neural Information Processing Systems (NIPS)*, pages 1038–1044, 1996.

[SV05]   Matthijs T. J. Spaan and Nikos Vlassis. Perseus: Randomized point-based value iteration for pomdps. *Journal of Machine Learning Research*, 24:195–220, 2005.

[Tes94]   Gerald Tesauro. Td-gammon, a self-teaching backgammon program, achieves masterlevel play. *Neural Computation*, 6(2):215–219, 1994.

[TR05]   Stephan Timmer and Martin Riedmiller. Learning policies for abstract states. In *Proceedings of the International Conference on Systems, Man and Cybernetics (SMC), Big Island, USA*, volume 4, pages 3179–3184, 2005.

[TR07a]   Stephan Timmer and Martin Riedmiller. Fitted q-iteration with cmacs. In *Proceedings of the International Symposium on Approximate Dynamic Programming and Reinforcement Learning (AD-PRL)*, pages 1–8, 2007.

[TR07b]   Stephan Timmer and Martin Riedmiller. Safe Q-Learning on Complete History Spaces. In *Proceedings of the 11th European Conference on Machine Learning (ECML), Warsaw, Poland*, 2007.

[Wat89]   Christopher Watkins. *Learning from Delayed Rewards*. PhD thesis, Cambridge University, Cambridge, England, 1989.

[Wil92]   Ronald J. Williams. Simple statistical gradient-following algorithms for connectionist reinforcement learning. *Machine Learning*, 8:229–256, 1992.

[ZZ01]   Nevin L. Zhang and Weihong Zhang. Speeding up the convergence of value iteration in partially observable markov decision processes. *Journal of Machine Learning Research*, 14:29–51, 2001.

Die VDM Verlagsservicegesellschaft sucht für wissenschaftliche Verlage abgeschlossene und herausragende

Dissertationen, Habilitationen, Diplomarbeiten, Master Theses, Magisterarbeiten usw.

für die kostenlose Publikation als Fachbuch.

Sie verfügen über eine Arbeit, die hohen inhaltlichen und formalen Ansprüchen genügt, und haben Interesse an einer honorarvergüteten Publikation?

Dann senden Sie bitte erste Informationen über sich und Ihre Arbeit per Email an *info@vdm-vsg.de*.

Sie erhalten kurzfristig unser Feedback!

VDM Verlagsservicegesellschaft mbH
Dudweiler Landstr. 99
D - 66123 Saarbrücken
www.vdm-vsg.de

Telefon +49 681 3720 174
Fax   +49 681 3720 1749

Die VDM Verlagsservicegesellschaft mbH vertritt

Printed by Books on Demand GmbH, Norderstedt / Germany